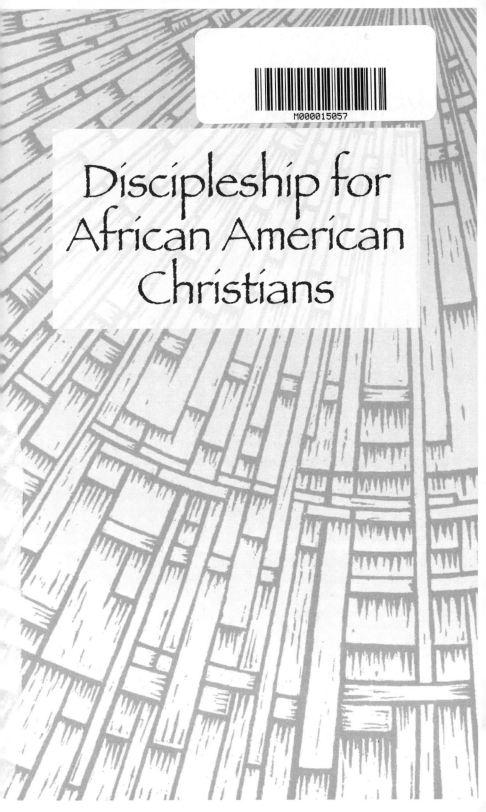

Discipleship for African American Christians

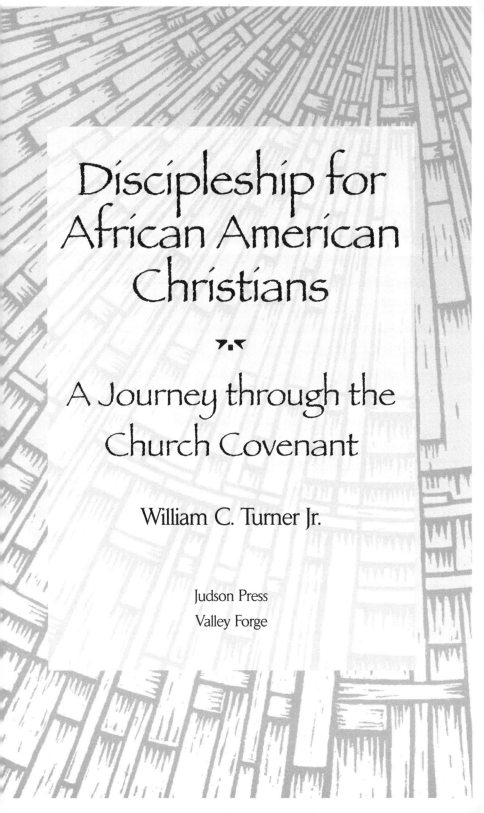

Discipleship for African American Christians

7.⊼

A Journey through the Church Covenant

William C. Turner Jr.

Judson Press
Valley Forge

Discipleship for African American Christians
A Journey through the Church Covenant
© 2002 by Judson Press, Valley Forge, PA 19482-0851
All rights reserved.

Unless otherwise indicated, Bible quotations in this volume are from The Holy Bible, King James Version. Other quotations, marked NIV, are from HOLY BIBLE: New International Version, copyright © 1973, 1978, 1984. Used by permission of Zondervan Bible Publishers.

Library of Congress Cataloging-in-Publication Data

Turner, William Clair, 1948-
    Discipleship for African American Christians : a journey through the church covenant / William C. Turner, Jr.
        p. cm.
    Includes bibliographical references.
    ISBN 0-8170-1434-9 (pbk. : alk. paper)
        1. African Americans—Religion—Sermons. 2. Baptists—Sermons.
    3. Sermons, American—20th century. 4. Christian life—Sermons.
    I. Title.

BR563.N4 .T86 2002
252'.06134—dc21   2002141553

Printed in the U.S.A.

16 15 14 13 12 11 10

10 9 8 7 6 5 4 3 2

Table of Contents

Church Covenant

HAVING BEEN LED, AS WE BELIEVE, BY THE SPIRIT OF GOD to receive the Lord Jesus Christ as our Saviour; and on the profession of our faith, having been baptized in the name of the Father, and of the Son, and of the Holy Spirit, we do now in the presence of God, angels and this assembly, most solemnly and joyfully enter into covenant with one another, as one body in Christ.

We engage, therefore, by the aid of the Holy Spirit, to walk together in Christian love; to strive for the advancement of this church in knowledge and holiness; to give it a place in our affections, prayers and services above every organization of human origin; to sustain its worship, ordinances, discipline and doctrine; to contribute cheerfully and regularly, as God has prospered us, towards its expenses, for the support of a faithful and evangelical ministry among us, the relief of the poor and the spread of the Gospel throughout the world. In case of difference of opinion in the church, we will strive to avoid a contentious spirit, and if we cannot unanimously agree, we will cheerfully recognize the right of the majority to govern.

We also engage to maintain family and secret devotion; to study diligently the word of God; to religiously educate our children; to seek the salvation of our kindred and acquaintance; to walk circumspectly in the world; to be kind and just to those in our employ, and faithful in the service we promise others; endeavoring in the purity of heart and good will towards all men to exemplify and commend our holy faith.

We further engage to watch over, to pray for, to exhort and stir up each other unto every good word and work; to guard each other's reputation, not needlessly exposing the infirmities of others; to participate in each other's joys, and with tender sympathy bear one another's burdens and sorrows; to cultivate Christian courtesy; to be slow to give or take offense, but always ready for reconciliation, being mindful of the rules of the Saviour in the eighteenth chapter of Matthew, to secure it without delay; and through life, amid evil report, and good report, to seek to live to the glory of God, who hath called us out of darkness into his marvelous light.

When we remove from this place, we engage as soon as possible to unite with some other church where we can carry out the spirit of this covenant and the principles of God's word.

Covenant Introduction

What one finds in the pages that follow is a collection of theological essays with subjects taken from the Covenant printed in the front of the *National Baptist Standard Hymnal*. Originally crafted as sermons, they were preached during regular Sunday morning worship at the Mount Level Missionary Baptist Church in Durham, North Carolina. I wondered whether the interest of the congregation could be sustained over the period of time required for such a challenging (or should I say bold) venture. My deepest fear was that somewhere along the way the people would get tired and stop coming or that the deacons would bring me back to reality, saying, "Pastor, don't you think you have dealt with this topic enough?" To my amazement, the interest not only remained high; it increased. While knowing what the next topic would be, the congregants continued to come, and services continued to be times of great celebration. Let me state as clearly as possible the several reasons for undertaking this task.

Pastoral and Teaching Needs

The project began with my efforts in a class offered to new members. Seeing no acceptable instructional materials for them (or, that is, knowing of none), I began teaching directly from the Covenant. I knew the Covenant well but had never heard exposition on it. In the Baptist church in the community where I was reared, Providence Park in Richmond, Virginia, the reading of the Covenant was a regular part of worship on Communion Sunday. For a youngster like myself, committing it to memory was no difficult task. Rather, it was fun. I was never a formal member of this congregation. Nevertheless my family and the church mutually claimed each other. The members were as much my family as any church family can be, and the pastor was as much a pastor to me as a pastor can be. Indeed, the pastor of some thirty years, Miles J. Jones, came to install me in the church I presently serve.

What I decided to do for catechesis was to take a clause or two from the Covenant (never as much as a paragraph) and find corresponding scriptural references. From there I proceeded to instruct. In my immediate view were issues pertaining to the faith that every believer should know and understand. People need to know the basics of soteriology, or what it means to be saved. In particular, Baptists need to be keen on the relationship between baptism and salvation: the two are neither separable nor identical. The last thing I wanted to do was pull down some metatradition—as in what one finds on the television and in the popular media. The teaching needed to be related to the context in which people live and the tradition of faith in which they make the good confession and purpose to run the race with patience.

On occasion I invited deacons, other officers, and church members into the class. Discussion and interest were constantly high. Quite often the comment was made that this was teaching to which the entire church should be exposed. Some people could not recall being catechized in this manner upon their baptism or being received into the local assembly. Others observed that sessions of this sort would make a good refresher for everyone. After much thought and prayer, "it seemed good to the Holy Ghost and to us" (Acts 15:28) to make this the focus of preaching in the church for a season.

This project, growing out of my experience as the pastor of a Baptist congregation, is very much related to some other factors as well. One is widespread fascination with Word ministries that pride themselves on teaching, as opposed to the traditional preaching of the black church or the caricature of it. Among these teachers there has been identification of the flaw in the sort of preaching that is more style than substance. This preaching is artistic, entertaining, and done in an idiom that is quite appealing to the emotions. Whooping, tuning, toning, and chanting are characteristic features of this style. It can be awesome in its power to move a congregation. Humor is often the byproduct or aftermath when substance is woefully lacking. The joke is sometimes told of persons who exclaimed, "Reverend surely did preach!" When asked what he said, they are reported to have said, "I don't know what he talked about, but he preached mighty good." My conviction is that the form of preaching does not make the content bad. Similarly, the form of teaching does not make the content good. Whatever is done under either the label of preaching or teaching is bad if it is careless theologically.

A deliberate decision reflected in this project is to work critically and constructively within the tradition. This approach is an alternative to the attempt of those involved with Word ministries who obscure the tradition informing their theology. The same range of teaching done by others is found among Word teachers: they have their theology, their hermeneutics, their social location, their privileged texts, and their social vision. But it is packaged as the Word in such a manner as to feign a pristine purity that no teaching in our time can possibly have. Some of the traditions reflected in this teaching are Pentecostal, fundamentalist, Christian Science, old-fashioned racism and white supremacy, and a radically conservative political agenda. Presentation as the Word prescinds any sort of challenge and compels obedience from those who are persuaded.

These essays take clearly recognized issues from the tradition of black Baptist churches as their anchor. I say black Baptist churches fully recognizing that this Covenant is cherished by more than those who are Baptists in the formal sense. I also recognize that covenants are not the unique property of black Baptists—covenants are commonplace among all Baptists and other Christians as well. Using the Covenant as the point of departure reflects the theological move within black churches where the content delivered is adapted (signified upon) to meet the needs of the people. While it is true that in the eyes of some this move may not be Afrocentric, it must be said in response that this is the way the theological task is undertaken in black churches, and finally, this method is more recognizable than others.

Source of Theology and Instruction in Baptist Churches

Phrasing the issue another way: I have seen Baptist students in theology become no less than frustrated when asked to pursue a theological issue (or do theology) from within their tradition. This is not to say that Baptists don't do theology. There are no believers or other religious persons in such a category. One could go so far as to say that such a position is fictitious. Theology, or reasoning about God, is an activity in which any person devoted to God participates. What one is hard pressed to find among Baptists is theology as a scientific discipline. By this I mean theology that discloses its sources in Scripture, tradition, reason, and experience and attempts to give an account of how these sources are utilized in the process of reflection.

The essays contained herein are in large measure illustrative of a way of doing theology that takes seriously the immediate and long-standing tradition in which believers stand. This is an attempt to correct the problem wherein tradition is shorn from its roots in Scripture and the reflective life of the church. The result is that some content of tradition is regarded as tradition alone, with no sense of how it is rooted in Scripture. This is surely the case with much of the Covenant among those who know it but are scripturally illiterate. Another way of putting the matter is this: I have juxtaposed factors crucial to life within a covenant community and the Scriptures that give authority to that covenant. Phrases from the Covenant supply topics, and reflection upon the appropriate texts of Scripture supplies the discourse.

This book addresses a further problem in this regard. Baptists represent a wing of the Reformation that had little regard for creeds, dogmatic treatises, and systematic theology. This was understandable due in large measure to the persecution suffered under the auspices of established religion. The history of Baptists was painful under the Roman Catholics during periods of inquisition and the stamping out of so-called enthusiasts, who were accused of being heretics. Essentially these were the persons who dared to challenge the authority of the hierarchy and magisterium. Persecution was similarly suffered at the hands of Protestant reformers who became established in the sense that they received protection through the might of the princes and the army. The memory of such persecution lives long.

The problem is that Baptist roots within the larger Reformation tradition are often obscured. This vital link severed, no connection can be seen with the larger history of interpretation within the church. Insistence is on believers' baptism, what constitutes ordinance (rather than sacraments), and the form of government (ecclesiology) and differentiating marks of Baptists. However, on a host of other issues (the Trinity, the place of Scripture, soteriology, etc.) Baptist faith is Reformed faith. There is tremendous value in viewing and tracking the church within this historical tradition.

The writing contained herein is written intentionally as a theology for African American Baptists. It is a theology of Covenant and community. Its deliberate intent is to make explicit the factors that are essential for living together as people of the Covenant—people who have no authority other than the Covenant to hold them together. It is done in the style of earlier theologies, such as those of Augustine, Calvin, Luther, Wesley, and Richard Allen, where the argument is rested in Scripture. Or, one may speak even more historically of the catechetical style of the early church, where a series of lectures was presented to those who offered themselves to be united with the church. Here I specifically have in mind Cyril of Jerusalem, whose catechetical lectures are something of a model within the church for how persons are instructed in the faith.

The Christian Right and the African American Church

Another vexing issue, which may be even more crucial, is the increasing influence from the Christian Right on African American Christians. Conservative by nature, the black church is easily enamored of those who use the same soteriological (having to do with the theology of salvation or how we are saved) language and appear to possess the same or similar spirituality. Unknown to many is the extent to which this brand of conservative evangelicalism is the bearer of contemporary racism that has black people working against their best interests and the best interests of others who are poor or marginalized within the culture.

To a large degree, the Christian Right carries over the tradition that defended slavery, redeemed the South, inaugurated Jim Crow, and upbraided the Declaration of Independence as an "infidel pestilence." In many ways, this is the religion of the lost cause. This gospel, in summary, is that God did not make all people equal: some were created by God to be the hewers of wood and the drawers of water, and seeking to change one's station is a violation of eternal decree. In the twentieth century, America has been in one long liberal funk that is bringing the nation to the precipice of destruction. A new redemption is required that will conserve the moral fabric. Returning black people to their right place is surely a part of the scheme that promises to carry the nation back to a time of pristine purity—a time preceding the New Deal, the Great Society, the civil rights movement, and social equality for women.

Specific issues that remain atop this political agenda are the fights against abortion, homosexuality, sex education, and the like. The support is for prayer in schools, the right to carry guns without restriction, capital punishment, reforms that devastate the poor, and an end to affirmative action. There is opposition to nearly every form of social program that would assist the downtrodden. Returning America back to God is not separable, these leaders would have one think, from the conservative agenda.

The leaders of this movement (television preachers are perhaps the most well-known of the lot) define salvation so as to produce robotlike repeaters of the party line. Invariably this nurture is productive of defense of the status quo and palliative for those who are not comfortable with the content of the spoon feeding. As in slavery, salvation is construed as the remedy for the "unruly Negroes" who could not otherwise be brought in without a tragedy of sorts. Language and forms of worship endemic to the black church can be heard coming from the lips of those who would prefer seeing the historic black churches shut their doors.

Pentecostal-Charismatic Internal Critique

There is a deliberate attempt in what follows to highlight the pneumatocentric (Holy Spirit–centered) character of historic Baptist faith. This applies especially to the doctrine of salvation (soteriology) and the doctrine of the church (ecclesiology). Each of the four major paragraphs in the Covenant begins by referencing the Spirit as the power that makes compliance with the Covenant possible. One is "led" by the Spirit to receive the Lord Jesus and enter into Covenant. One "engages" by the aid of the Spirit to walk together in Christian love. The Spirit is the antecedent for those matters wherein the covenanting person "also engages" and "further engages." Without the Spirit the Covenant falls apart, salvation loses all its meaning, and the church disintegrates into a collection of individuals. Indeed, the history of the church is littered with the corpses of those who, for forgetting the Spirit, brought this doom on themselves and their offspring. This utter reliance on the Spirit is easily lost in the establishment of the church or in those hegemonic contexts where there is overreliance on the culture for legitimacy and sanction.

Black Baptists and most African American Christians have been forced to rely on power not derived from the formal sources of authority within the culture. The power works from within—like dynamite (dunamis). This is charismatic power—the power of the Spirit. Where churches remain vibrant and healthy, there is utter and complete reliance on the Spirit. When this reliance is forgotten, it is soon relearned where churches remain in viable competition for the souls sought by the drug lords.

What one will find in these essays is sensitivity to issues of pneumatology (theology of the Holy Spirit) raised in Holiness-Pentecostal-charismatic circles. This move accomplishes two purposes: it makes the pneumatology within the Baptist tradition explicit, and it offers a critique from within the larger tradition of the church for some of the untested claims of newer, more radical positions. Repeatedly the discussion follows the Scriptures closely and scrupulously. Even where there is reference to tradition, the Scripture gives the grounding.

The Regenerate African American

The question that haunts me in this project is the one with which I have been wrestling for years: What does the regenerate African American look like as we enter the twenty-first century? This is not a moot or idle question. It is clear that from the early days of American civilization this was an issue over which there was considerable debate. For some, the regenerate African American was one who was persuaded by the gospel to become the best slave the master could own. The Christian slave was to be the model. Most of all, he or she was not to take baptism and admission to the Lord's Table as an occasion to sue for political and social freedom. The claim of the New Testament that there is neither Jew nor Greek, bond nor free, in Christ was taken to mean that the gospel of liberty in the Spirit had nothing to do with one's temporal condition. God was said to have ordained the states in which persons were historically found, and to tamper with those states was a violation of providence.

African American Christians saw the matter in the opposite way. Indeed, they were more in line with the tradition of the church, that Christians do not and must not hold one another in bondage. Confessions of faith in Christ meant automatic release from physical bondage.

Sadly, it must be acknowledged that the clarity of previous generations concerning the vocation of African American Christians has been lost to a large degree. Few forums exist for hammering out a behavior consistent with emancipated persons—that is, a liberative praxis. Sainted forbearers who served God while they or their fellows were in chains understood the vocation clearly. They were to struggle against the avaricious demon with all the power God gave. The struggle could take the form of preaching and protest, it could consist of escaping bondage and manumitting others, it could be a physical struggle with the oppressor, or it could be quiet prayer while passing the torch of resistance to another generation.

Similarly, in the epochs following emancipation and reconstruction, Jim Crow, civil rights, and black power, there was a more or less common wisdom concerning what was our calling under God. This common wisdom informed the way parents and communities nurtured children, the way people were prodded to live productive lives, and the way codes of respect were set in place and observed. Boundaries of decency existed within even the "roughest communities." With the collapse of these structures and the erosion of their foundations, there must be deliberate attention to the details of living in community. Assumptions can no longer be made concerning what people ought to know when it comes to issues of ethics, morality, courtesy, kindness, and honor. This truth applies even within the church. A new era of teaching—much like the one that followed emancipation—is in order. This extended essay intends to be part of that project.

Focused by Reality

It should also be noted that these lessons were developed during a normal cycle of life within the church—and within a black Baptist church, specifically. It could be argued that the focus in these essays is too narrow. I have already spoken to the possible value they may have to non-Baptists. But what might be their value to non-African Americans? Here I invoke the Les McCann principle—if you are trying to make it real, you must answer the question "Compared with what?" Too often in doing theology the particular "what" has been obscured, leaving a universal fuzziness.

My experience as a teacher of theology, preaching, and black church studies convinces me beyond any doubt that focusing on the what of African American experience does not limit the value of the reflection or instruction. Applications from the life of the African American church make some of the best data for studying theology in North America. If anything, a focus on African American experience broadens the range and relevance. It reveals the suppressed self-consciousness of the larger culture and exposes the self-knowledge of African Americans.

1

We Enter into Covenant

Lesson: 1 Peter 2:1-10

But ye are a chosen generation, a royal priesthood, an holy nation, a peculiar people; that ye should show forth the praises of him who hath called you out of darkness into his marvelous light; which in time past were not a people, but are now the people of God; which had not obtained mercy, but now have obtained mercy. (1 PETER 2:9-10)

"We do now in the presence of God ... enter into covenant with one another, as one body in Christ."

This is the first in a series of lessons that explores what it means to be a Christian congregation, a family of believers. We are an ecclesia, a gathered community, those who have been called out from among the world to be the body of Christ in this location. We will examine together the content of instruction that is given to new members. On more than one occasion some who are not so new have noted that this

1

instruction is good for us all. Periodically it is good to review what makes us who we are and what gives us our identity.

Note that our focus is the church covenant. We read it from time to time, but its value extends far beyond the mere reading of the words. The Covenant is the means by which we affirm the identity God has given us. We have no other account of ourselves. We reject the notion that the authority for our existence as a family lies with temporal powers. We do not exist by the will of the government. Although its sanction is cherished, we would not cease to exist if the church were declared illegal. Neither do we depend on magistrates to protect us in the teaching we give, the witness we make to the world, or the sanctions placed upon those who choose to travel this way. What's more, no other ecclesiastical body outside this congregation can superimpose an authority to order the way we live out our commitment to Christ. We exist as a community of believers by virtue of the covenant into which we have entered in the presence of God and by the leading of the Holy Spirit.

It is good that we are beginning reflection today. This is the first Sunday in the new year. There is no better way to begin than by rehearsing who we are under God. Many other interests will define us if we are not clear who we are under God. Conveniently, we are often defined in this culture by our race. We stand out because of the color of our skin and the meaning that has been placed on the fact of difference within this civilization. Along with the fact of our color is a history of oppression, suppression, reaction, and struggle. If we allow it, we can be defined by our economic status or the section of town in which we live. Or we can be defined by denomination and traditional factors that begin with and magnify our lack of continuity with others who are in the body of Christ. But what we cherish far more on this day is that we are those whom God has permitted to see one more day in the year of the Lord.

No word of Scripture is clearer in telling us what it means to be in a covenant community than the one found in 1 Peter 2. In coming to terms with the meaning of a Christian community, the epistle writer probes the critical dialectic of our identity. On the one hand are the discrete members constituting the community; on the other hand is the community as a spiritual entity that cannot be reduced to its constituents. It is almost like the chicken and the egg: one is hard pressed to say which came first. Without the chicken there are no eggs; without the eggs there are no chickens. Without believers there is no covenant community, but without the covenant community there are no believers.

See how Peter shows the interconnection: the community is likened to a spiritual house built of stones. These are living stones; they give life to the edifice. The materials within a building have limited value outside of the structure. Put another way, the church has no life without lively members, and the members have limited life apart from a lively church. In the final analysis we are hard pressed to say what has top priority: those within the church, or the church comprised of those who have entered into covenant.

We deliberately do not speak of individuals, as this contradicts the meaning of being a covenant community. Individualism as a philosophy is rooted in the false doctrine of human autonomy. In this false notion, each ego, or each private, knowing self, stands at the center of its own world. Identity is established by difference, distinction, standing over against other selves—by dominating other selves. That is the source of contrariness—being different for the sake of being different, being hard to get along with so somebody will acknowledge us, protesting merely for the sake of having power.

In the covenant community the primary, irreducible identity is persons being led by the Spirit into communion with other persons in whom the Spirit is performing the same saving work. There is no identity more rudimentary than entering into covenant. What we might otherwise call individuality is the sacrifice we bring to the God who calls us out of darkness, making us lively stones in the house the Spirit is fashioning.

We are also *a chosen generation.* That is, the primary datum of our reality is not by our initiative or our decision but the act of God. God's choice is the first and foremost factor. This knowledge serves to correct the notion that we can get saved when we get ready and that we can put our religion down when it is inconvenient or when the demands of our stewardship require behavior we do not prefer. We are chosen in Christ Jesus before the foundation of the world. We are begotten by the Word, born of the incorruptible seed that lives and abides forever (John 15:16; Ephesians 1:4; 1 Peter 1:23).

The call of God is effective in producing the response of faith, but God's choice is the decisive factor of our identity (Romans 11:29). Nothing else makes us the people of God. Obedience to God and love for one another sustain the relationship, but the choice of God initiates the covenant and gives it integrity. It is true that we bring the particulars of our identity with us, but the particulars can push us apart just as they bind us together. The tie that binds our hearts in Christian love, the fellowship of kindred minds, comes from above.

See how the new Israel is contrasted with the old. Under the old covenant, Israel consisted of the descendants of Abraham. Specifically they traced their identity through the line that narrowed, working its way through the seed of Isaac and Jacob. From all the families of the earth they were chosen, and the announcement was made in the scene when they stood before the flames and thunder that came from Sinai. But here we have a new generation; there is a new principle for the gathering of this community. The call of God is met by faith in Jesus as the Christ, the Son of the living God. It is a response to the gospel that invites whosoever will to come, to take up the cross and follow Jesus as a disciple (Galatians 2:17-20).

The choice of God does not make us better than others, giving us the right to look down upon or disparage those whom God is seeking. The call is to be a light, an example of what God can do with dust that is yielded to the divine hands. It is evidence of what the potter can do with broken vessels. The result of God's choice reinforces the awareness of our relative state without the choice of God: we would still be no people.

We are *a royal priesthood*. We are recipients of an anointing that authorizes us to rule and serve God's creation. We are to lead the creation in obedience to God, demonstrating the love God has for the world. The Son has offered perfect obedience, and by the anointing of the Spirit that same obedience is given to us.

The anointing that was reserved in former times for priests and kings is now upon all who respond to the call of God and yield their lives. The chief characteristic of the anointing was its fragrance. Blended in the manner of perfume, it contained cinnamon, cassia, aromatic cane, and myrrh mixed with olive oil. Pungent, strong in odor, it could not be missed or mistaken when it saturated the garment of the king or priest on whom it was poured (Exodus 30:31-38). Similarly, the Spirit is poured on us to give a powerful fragrance in a world choking from the stench of sin and powerless to return to God by its own might.

We need not come from a particular lineage, we do not need a certain family name, and there is no requirement of any certain biological pedigree. All are eligible to rule and serve in the name of the Lord. This priesthood does not belong to any family; it is the priesthood of Christ. Jesus Christ, the priest and sacrifice, offered himself upon the heavenly altar as the full, perfect, and sufficient sacrifice. Standing in the virtue of the priesthood, each believer can make an offering to God. Boldly we can approach the throne of grace in the time of need, and this we must all learn to do if we are to grow in grace (Hebrews 4:14-16). But each believer is also granted the authority of a priest to make intercession for another. In interceding with God for those who are lost, in bearing the burden of the one who needs strength, we strengthen the covenant community and cooperate with God in the work of redemption.

We are a holy nation. This means in Christ all that would otherwise distinguish us has been sanctified. We are taken just as we are. God does not require us to give up our culture, our talents, or the traits that distinguish us as persons to become like others. We are given power to be children of God (John 1:1-2; 1 John 1:1-4). Inwardly we are set free from the passions and desires that displease God, and outwardly our behavior is brought in conformity to the law of Christ.

What it means to be a holy nation once again relates to the image of the priest and king. They were set apart by the beauty of their presence. Theirs were not ordinary garments. At their investiture, mundane clothing was removed. Royal, purple, flowing vestments made of the finest cloth bedecked the king, and a crown speckled with the finest gems was placed upon his head. So ornate was the king's attire that no one could mistake his presence. Similarly with the priest: ordinary garments were removed. In their place were finely woven garments of fine linen and the striking colors of blue, scarlet, and purple. Precious gems decorated him, and on his head was a mitre inscribed in the center with the words "Holiness to the Lord" (Exodus 28:36). There is a beauty that God has ordained to be manifested in the covenant community as a holy nation. It is the beauty of the devoted and consecrated life. It is nothing short of beautiful to see how God takes us with all our differences, all of our shortcomings, and fashions a people for divine praise. This is the beauty of those who love and care for one another, and it is the beauty of those who care for the world.

We are a peculiar people. That is, we are precious in God's sight. For this, God has promised to care for us and defend us. There is nothing quite like us on this side of eternity. Indeed, we take our identity and the insight for our way of living from an order that has no precedence in history. In the strictest sense, it is hard for Christians to be conservative, because eyes have not seen the good things God has in store for us and what God is making of us. Consciously, intentionally, deliberately, we set our affection on things above and consider ourselves citizens of heaven. But we do this for the purpose of living to please God in the world. We see the world not merely as it has been or as it is, but as what it is being transformed into by God (1 Corinthians 15:24-25).

We bring ourselves, sinners who have been saved, filthy rags that have been washed, marred pots that have been crushed and remolded, prodigals who have been lost and found (Isaiah 64:6; Jeremiah 18:4; Luke 15:11-24). Some were dedicated from the cradle, but they still know they have not been preserved by their righteousness. Some possess one gift; others possess another. But all the gifts are brought together that in the spiritual house an acceptable sacrifice may be offered to God by Jesus Christ.

Our purpose beyond all others is to offer praise to God. We may do many other things, but we risk missing our calling if focus is ever lost on our central work. Indeed, this focus must be the thread that runs through and purifies everything we do. When we gather together, the place from which the Word is preached and the altar of sacrifice form the centerpiece. We are people who live in communion with Christ, feasting on the Word and being cleansed by the blood. Our mission is to share this communion with the world and to return for celebration of the great things God has done.

Like it or not, that makes us peculiar. We are different from the community club; our choir is different from a performing group; the boards are not another version of business corporations. We are a peculiar people, called to show forth the praises of the one who has called us out of darkness into the marvelous light. We dare to walk in the light, a beautiful light, and come where the dewdrops of mercy shine bright.

➤∎◄

For Reflection and Discussion

■ Put in your own words what it means to be a chosen generation, a royal priesthood, a holy nation, and a peculiar people.

2

Led to Receive the Lord Jesus

Lesson: Romans 8:1-14

For as many as are led by the Spirit of God, they are the sons [children] of God. (ROMANS 8:14)

▼.▼

"Having been led ... by the Spirit of God to receive the Lord Jesus Christ as our Savior...."

As members of the covenant community, we are led by the Spirit to receive the Lord Jesus as Savior. This is the common ground on which we stand as we enter into covenant. Erosion of this ground leaves us with no place to stand, for all other ground is sinking sand.

We do not place confidence in good will toward one another, for this can rise or fall. Nor can we place our faith with a political party or in economic security. Both can come and go. Friendships can fall apart, families feud, business partnerships go sour. But the ground on which we stand in Christ is solid. Without this ground all else is washed away (Luke 6:46-49).

We are led to receive Christ by the Spirit. Here, faith is the source of our knowledge. By faith we have a form of knowledge that is just as valid as other forms. Faith is a gift of the Spirit; it is the means by which we grasp the truth God is pleased to offer (Hebrews 11:6; Romans 10:17; 1 Corinthians 12:9). This truth concerns mysteries we cannot reach with our reason and cannot bring down to our terms. We receive from God the knowledge of how we are led into communion with Christ, restored to fellowship with God, and bound in covenant with others who believe. Without this faith it is impossible to please God. It is given to us through hearing the Word of God, and it is sufficient to ground us in the knowledge of God. In walking with Christ and with one another, faith is increased. Doubt is overcome, and we grow in grace.

Faith in some form exists in all endeavors. The mathematician cannot count or prove theorems without faith in the associative, commutative, and other mathematical properties. A doctor cannot make a diagnosis without faith that X-rays and other diagnostic procedures have yielded accurate results. And we cannot enter into covenant unless we believe that we, along with our brothers and sisters, are being led by the Spirit of God.

A lack of trust in the leading of the Spirit cripples our walk with God and our fellowship with others. The Covenant affirms our confidence in the promises of God. And if we have truly trusted God for our salvation, we can believe the same concerning others. If our trust is only halfhearted, we are prone to believe that way about others. But if we believe we are all under divine leading, we can love and trust as brothers and sisters, knowing we are subject to the same God who rules our life.

It cannot be overstated that the Covenant becomes effective through the Spirit. Such phrases as "led by the Spirit" and "we engage, therefore, by the aid of the Spirit" are in the present tense. Without the Spirit we have no communion with God and no genuine community among one another. In such a state we are no more than a collection of egos going separate ways.

How are we led by the Spirit? Romans 8:14 states that as many as are led by the Spirit of God are the sons (children) of God. Being led by the Spirit means being open to a special relationship with God, a relationship that God initiates. Through this relationship, God nurtures us, guides us, forms us into the image of Christ, making us partakers of the divine nature.

But in this case, the purpose for the Spirit's leading is specific. That purpose is to receive the Lord Jesus as our personal Savior. This is the focal point of our faith. Specific choices that open into the ways of life or death are directly influenced by the choice we make in this grand moment of being led by the Spirit. It is a moment wrapped in eternity. It is the moment in which the Spirit is the witness to what has been told us about Christ and prompts our spirit to respond, "Yes, I believe."

The Spirit is the witness. Like the eyewitness on the stand in the courtroom, the Spirit testifies to our hearts telling us that the good news of the gospel is true. There were numerous witnesses to the death of Christ on the cross. There were many witnesses who claimed they saw the risen Lord. But the Holy Spirit is the witness who verifies that the Son was sent into the world as the expression of God's love and for the express purpose of restoring us to fellowship. The Holy Spirit is the witness to the powers of sin being broken and the sting of death being removed. This heavenly witness testifies to all who will hear that the gospel is true.

The Spirit convicts us, convinces us that we are lost without God's provision, that we cannot live right on our own (John 15:26-27; 16:8-11). There is no need to doubt the gospel; the Spirit testifies that it is true.

Being led to receive Jesus is not the end of something but the beginning of a process of sanctification. It is like deciding to travel north on the interstate instead of south. It determines the community into which we are incorporated by means of covenant. It is the tie that binds our hearts in fellowship by divine power.

Our mothers and fathers in the faith had a way of accenting the critical nature of this moment. No matter when you made up your mind to follow Jesus, you announced that choice at the mourners' bench—usually during revival. In some cases the mourners' bench was the time to persuade persons that this was the right choice. Our eternal destiny was mapped before us, and there was no lack of clarity concerning how crucial the choice was. But with or without the bench, this is the degree of seriousness with which we are dealing.

Accepting Christ is a choice a person must make in order to participate in the covenant community in any meaningful way. With children we may make exception for the purpose of leading them to commitment. But grown folk ought to know by now what they want to do—whether to follow Jesus, straddle the fence, or worse.

The Spirit leads us to receive the Lord Jesus as our Savior. And what a joyful sound it is to hear that Jesus saves. From A to Z, Jesus saves. Jesus saves from anxieties, burdens, carnality; from drugs, emptiness, and frustration; from peer pressure, quarrelsome patterns, and roguish ways; from vileness, wickedness, and X-rated corruption. In short, Jesus saves us from sin and into a new way of life. Accepting this salvation lies at the center, the core of our faith.

For Reflection and Discussion

- In the process of receiving Christ, what is the relationship between God's role and our role?
- Put in your own words how a decision to accept Christ should influence the way a person lives, thinks, and feels.
- Describe the time in your life when you made a decision to receive Christ. How has it made a difference for you?

₃ 3 ₓ

The Profession of Faith and Baptism

Lessons: Mark 16:15-16; Romans 6:1-11;
1 Peter 3:21; 1 Corinthians 12:12

Therefore we are buried with him by baptism into death: that like as Christ was raised up from the dead by the glory of the Father, even so we also should walk in newness of life. (ROMANS 6:4)

"On the profession of our faith, having been baptized...."

The Covenant into which we enter and which establishes us before God as a community of believers requires a personal profession of faith and a conscious decision to be baptized. Christ offers salvation through godly parents who dedicate children to God and nurture them in the fear of the Lord. But this gift can be denied. To join the community of believers, a person must make a profession of saving faith—by his or her volition—and receive baptism.

Baptism should not be considered the equivalent of receiving Jesus as Savior. A person can come to belief in the quietness of the home or the heart. Conversion can take place in the pew or the parking lot. We learn in Ephesians 2:8-9 that salvation and regeneration occur in God's time and in God's way. But to profess faith publicly makes a person accountable for the decision to accept Christ. It brings faith out of the corner, out of the closet.

Baptism constitutes a public profession of faith. It represents the New Testament pattern: believe and be baptized. This is what Peter told those convicted by his teaching on the Day of Pentecost. It is also the response of the Ethiopian eunuch, who, upon reading the scroll of Isaiah, asked, "What doth hinder me to be baptized?" (Acts 8:36). Although biblical exceptions to this pattern do exist (e.g., the thief on the cross who believed but had no opportunity to be baptized), when coming to terms with the meaning of baptism we do not start with exceptional cases. Rare exceptions to the prevailing principle fail to disclose the meaning of this great gift of God to those who believe.

Since the essential meaning of baptism is spiritual, insight is given in the Scriptures by means of images rooted in the story of salvation. These images enable us to see in figures what God accomplishes in the believing soul that is joined to Christ. These images also require retelling the good news of salvation, which is God's marvelous work that reconciles the world. These images further prompt us to tell the story of how we have been apprehended by God's grace and made joint heirs with Christ (Romans 8:17).

You see, professing faith and baptism go together. In the Great Commission, our Lord enjoins us to make disciples and to baptize. Of course such a command entails many things, but there is little else that we are directly instructed to do as we go forth in the name of the Lord.

In the New Testament church, a public profession of faith was no light matter. It was how people identified with a new way of living. It broke indecision and aligned men and women with the way of the Messiah, the way of suffering. It put them in line to be victims of persecution. Today, baptism as the public profession of faith is a deliberate attempt to follow the New Testament pattern. It is full of intense meaning and should be considered among the most awe-inspiring moments in the life of any fellowship of believers.

The water used to baptize is no different from the water in the swimming pool or the shower. But the act of baptism takes on meaning because of its spiritual significance. Various images in the Scriptures provide insight into the spiritual meaning of baptism. These images, rooted in the story of salvation, appeal to our senses and enable us to understand more deeply what God accomplishes when the believing soul is joined to Christ. They require the retelling of the story of the gospel. But more, they prompt the telling of our story of how we have been apprehended by the grace of God and made joint heirs together with Christ (Romans 8:17).

In Romans 6, the apostle Paul offers the image of being buried and raised with Christ. Here baptism is linked to the gospel: Jesus died for our sins and rose in power. God offers new life and fellowship through the Son. Accordingly, baptism is a tangible expression, an offering of God's grace. In baptism, a person is received into the life of God in a manner similar to entering the water. He or she is received by God as by the water—fully, without fear or reservation.

The drama of baptism is built around Christ's death, burial, and resurrection into which we enter. The most radical work in baptism is done by the Holy Ghost, who does spiritually to our sinful self what has been done physically to an executed criminal. Dead persons are rendered incapable of committing the acts that once characterized them. The thief cannot steal; the murderer poses no threat. Baptism signifies deadness to the trespass. Baptized persons are no longer available as an instrument of unrighteousness. We are dead to sin. It has no power to re-enlist us as its slaves. The grace of being free from the shackles of sin is offered to us in baptism.

But not only are we dead to sin; we are alive to God. The tongue that once lied now offers praise to God. The mind that imagined wicked things now receives visions of service to God and blessings for fellow men and women. This newness of life is not fiction or fantasy: the change is recognizable by those who knew us previously. As our mothers and fathers in the faith put it, "I looked at my hands, and they looked new; I looked at my feet, and they did too. All around me looked so fine, till I asked my Lord if all was mine."

In 1 Peter 3:21, baptism is likened to entering the ark of safety, being rescued from the storm, saved from a world that has turned against God. This image provides a contrast between what it means to live in Christ and following the course of this world. In this image, baptism saves us. As with Noah's ark, God anticipates the destruction to which we are headed if we follow the course of this world. In a wicked, godless generation, God offers a safety zone. This safety zone is baptism.

Baptism is so much more than just saying no. It is a place to live under divine protection. For children, it might mean protection from peer pressure and courage to obey those who teach the right way. For adolescents, it might mean strength to stand against the dangers of drugs, fornication, destructive habits, and the temptation to waste God-given talent. For mothers, somewhere to go when nobody understands. For fathers, a friend to lean on when the load demands strength. For all, baptism offers peace in the midst of the storm.

As a bath washes us physically, baptism removes concupiscence—that is, the lust, the desire, the craving for what God forbids (Romans 7:8). Prior to this inner cleansing, we are bound and determined to have what God says we may not have and to do what God says we shall not do. But this inner washing leaves us with a new desire to please God.

Baptism offers security for our souls as we stay in the ark. We need God to stand by us when the storms of life are raging. It provides the assurance that when Jesus is the captain of this Old Ship of Zion, the water cannot harm us.

Paul offers a third image in 1 Corinthians 12:13, where water is a symbol of the Spirit and baptism is the drinking of that Spirit. The purpose of the Spirit, as it enters into us, is to take control and carry us fully into the life and will of God. God's intention is for all who are baptized to come under the full control of the Spirit. Continual drinking, sufficient to bring on intoxication, is the protocol for true believers.

Being baptized offers a new direction and an opportunity to begin again, whether we have strayed off course for a day, a month, or a year. We are constantly called to abide in our baptism, to remember that in its meaning are found comfort, strength, and hope.

For Reflection and Discussion

- What memories do you have about your baptism? How did it change your understanding of your Christian faith?
- Which of the three images—being buried and raised with Christ, being aboard the ark of safety, or drinking in the Spirit—means the most to you, and why?
- In the trials and temptations of everyday life, how might the memory of your baptism make a difference?

4

Baptized in the Name of the Father, and of the Son, and of the Holy Ghost

Lessons: Matthew 28:19-20; 1 John 5:5-14

For there are three that bear record in heaven, the Father, the Word [the Son], and the Holy Ghost: and these three are one. (1 JOHN 5:7)

"In the name of the Father, and of the Son, and of the Holy Spirit...."

What does it mean to be baptized in the name of the Father, and of the Son, and of the Holy Spirit? As we have already seen in the example of baptism itself, because of the limits of human speech and understanding, we must resort to images to articulate and confess divine reality and actions. What we have in this trinitarian formula is the church's way of confessing the mystery of God.

God is revealed as Father, Son, and Spirit. The living God exists from eternity in three persons. Divine persons are not to be confused with what we mean by individuals. Divine persons live in one another and possess equal power, glory, and holiness. They possess one will and do their distinctive work for one purpose. This is why Jesus could say, "I am in the Father and the Father is in me" (John 14:10) and why he went on to say the Spirit would glorify him by taking what is Jesus' and showing it to us, Christ's followers (John 16:14-15).

The focus of God's revelation is the Son, Jesus the Christ, who prays to the Father and who promises to send the Spirit (John 15:26). The Son came to earth as the expressed image of the invisible God. He is the brightness of God's glory. The Spirit came upon the Son at baptism and empowered the ministry of deliverance. Upon the return of the Son to the Father, the Spirit has been given for the life of the church and to empower all who believe (Hebrews 1:3; 9:13-14; 10:5).

The doctrine of the Trinity is sometimes misrepresented as a deep and great mystery from which believers should retreat into less complex realms of simple faith. The tragedy is that in such attempts at simplification we fail to confess the God who has been revealed. Instead, we confess a limited God. The doctrine of the Trinity allows us to confess precisely this mystery. It is the church's way of insisting that in all things we keep the mystery before us, not being seduced into reducing the eternal and all-wise God to the level of our limited reasoning and comprehension.

There are those who say the church should concern itself with the problems of the world instead of wasting time on mysterious doctrines. But these doctrines enable us to know and serve more fully the true and living God, providing a basis for the transforming witness that offers the world true hope.

In baptizing in the name of the Father, and of the Son, and of the Holy Spirit, we return glory to the Father who created us. We do this through the Son, who offered the sufficient sacrifice, and in the power of the Holy Spirit, who is given to be with us and in us. These three agree, having one mind, one will, and one purpose.

We are called by our baptism to glorify the Father, the source of all things. Out of love the Father created and continues to create. We confess that the heavens declare the glory of God; the firmament shows the glory of all the works of God's hands (Psalm 19:1). From the mouths of babes, God has ordained praise (Psalm 8:2). The trees of the woods and the mighty oceans are to praise the Lord (Psalm 148:7-9). Everything that has breath is to praise the Lord (Psalm 150:6), giving glory to the Father.

Marvelous clarity can come for us when we know our purpose for being in the world, and baptism in the name of the Father bestows this clarity and reveals the purpose of our existence. This clarity has implications for the details of our lives. We cannot separate glorifying the Father from caring for, rather than abusing, our bodies or from engaging our mental energies for constructive purposes rather than polluting the mind. In choosing friends, in making decisions concerning our work, in giving the kind rather than the vexing word, we must keep in mind the calling of our baptism to glorify the Father.

We who are baptized in the name of the Father are linked with God's redeeming purposes throughout history. We are joined with those who were baptized in the wilderness under the cloud as we move to the redemption God has ordained for the world. We may not understand every phase of the journey. Some details remain inscrutable. But we are enjoined to patiently wait on the Lord, for in all things we are called to glorify the Father (Psalm 27:14).

We are called also by our baptism to live in the obedience of the Son. The Son, who is begotten of the Father, is like the Father in eternity, wisdom, power, and holiness. Yet the Son is like the creation, having been given the power to go forth from and return glory to the Father. In the bosom of the Father from eternity, the Son took on the nature of the creature. Active in the work of creation, the Son upholds all things by the word of his power. Indeed, as the fourth Evangelist declares, "All things were made by him; and without him was not any thing made that was made" (John 1:3).

The Father gave us a gift of one who knew no sin, had no blemish, possessed no flaws, and was guilty of no faults. Through the Son the Father receives the obedience of all who would dare believe on Christ for salvation. To be baptized in the name of the Son means that God no longer looks on our state but at Christ, in whom our lives are hid (Colossians 3:1-2). The Father, who cannot embrace sin, allowed the Son to take it upon himself. He who knew no sin became sin (2 Corinthians 5:21) and paid the debt. And he bestows his sinless righteousness upon us.

Without faith, profession, and baptism into Christ, the debt would be ours to pay, the load would be ours to bear, and the death would be ours to die. Outside of Christ we must answer every infraction, repair every breech, make restitution for every injury, and re-establish peace with God. But being baptized into Christ's death means all that can be demanded of us has been paid in full. We've heard it said, "He paid a debt he did not owe; I owed a debt I could not pay."

Thus through our baptism in the name of the Son, we gain freedom, liberty. A yoke of bondage is removed. It is a yoke to which we need never again submit. We who have been baptized are to assert our freedom radically. We are not to be shy in rejecting bondage. Firmly, vigorously, with mighty protest, we are to refuse any yoke that would be set on our shoulders by any power. Nobody owns us now; the rights of all other masters are cancelled. Whether the threat comes from political, social, or economic camps, our answer is to be no to those masters and yes to the one who died for us. We can afford to be bold in the matter, for we are baptized in the one at whose name every knee must bow (Philippians 2:9-11).

And we are baptized in the name of the Holy Ghost, the Spirit of God who goes forth into the creation to give life, vitality, and power. The Spirit takes the virtue of all Christ has done in obedience to the Father and gives it to us. The Spirit proceeds from the depths of God as the very breath of life. Like fire, the Spirit purges, supplying energy and power. Like springs of living water, the Spirit nourishes and nurtures, keeping life fresh and exciting (Genesis 1:2).

We are baptized in the name and in the power of the Spirit of life. We do not remain buried and dead, even as Christ did not remain in the grave. When the sacrifice was offered to the Father, the Spirit quickened the lifeless form, raising him with power over death, hell, and the grave (Romans 8:11). All deadness, lethargy, powerlessness, and excuses have to go when the Spirit of life enters.

Life, vitality, and power. These are the marks of the Spirit and of our baptism. Baptized believers have as their first and foremost calling the worship and praise of God in spirit and truth. The pursuit of this calling is not bound by the limits of our humanity. It grows, it increases, and it shines in spite of historical and physical circumstances. It counters the forces of opposition, persecution, tribulation, and even death. Outwardly we may be perishing, but inwardly we are renewed

(2 Corinthians 4:13-16). By the power of the Spirit we are lifted as if on the wings of a dove and carried to a place of peace in the storm, quietness in the midst of turmoil, refreshment in the raging tide of life. The vitality of the Spirit carries us through death and brings us fully into the presence of the one who created us, regenerated us, and promised us full redemption. Indeed, the Spirit supplies the seal that keeps us and that shall identify us on that crowning day.

The pattern given in baptism applies to worship, service, fellowship, and all other things pertaining to our life in God. We glorify the Father through the Son in the power of the Spirit. In this trinitarian pattern, the entire drama of salvation is kept before us. It is a key to understanding what it means to have fellowship, communion with God, so that we might overcome the world. Thus we praise God from whom all blessings flow! We praise the Father, Son, and Holy Ghost!

➤.◆

For Reflection and Discussion

- Have you ever found the doctrine of the Trinity confusing? In what ways has this chapter helped to clarify your understanding?
- What are the common purposes of the Father, the Son, and the Holy Spirit?
- How do you live your life as a Christian as a result of having been freed from all yokes and burdens? What are the implications of that freedom?

5

We Solemnly and Joyfully Enter into Covenant

Lesson: Psalm 100

Know ye that the Lord he is God: ...we are his people, and the sheep of his pasture. (PSALM 100:3)

"We do now ... most solemnly and joyfully enter into covenant with one another, as one body in Christ."

Solemnity and joy may not be total opposites, but they are two words that don't normally go together. It is hard to imagine being solemn and joyful at the same time. But these words reflect a wide range of attitudes we bring to the Covenant.

That we enter into covenant solemnly suggests that it is a serious matter. Being bound in covenant is serious business largely because it is done in the presence of God and the angels. God is the witness to this union. It stands to reason that we will treat one another differently in light of a conscious awareness that God is watching. The same God who created us gives us one heart and one spirit. When we thwart this oneness, as we sometimes do, it is likewise serious business.

As the human body has vitality and harmony through the interdependence of its parts, systems, and joints, so the local church is made one through the dynamic diversity of its members. We must learn to take more seriously, more solemnly if you will, the acts that hold us together and that keep the covenant viable. We must recognize a relationship between building up the church's corporate life and nourishing personal life, even though there is not always an obvious personal benefit for everything we do to build up the Body. We will not last long in the Lord's service if we make our calculations thinking only about what is best for me. This principle applies to all relationships, including those in the realm of marriage and family.

Building up the common life is as serious and solemn a task in our time as it ever was. If we think we can make it on our own, it is time to think again. If we think we can escape fellow human beings and retreat into the tidy world of the nuclear family, we will be rudely awakened. For at some point we all need each other.

With this in mind, either we will love one another by the grace of God, or we will suffer degradation together. Martin Luther King Jr. was correct that we are bound together in a common web of destiny and we will either live together as brothers and sisters, or we will perish together as fools.

When we come together to worship we are building up the common life. Praise ascends from one life, one voice, and is co-mingled with the praise of others as the Spirit produces the atmosphere of rejoicing and refreshing. You can't sit back waiting for someone to sing or say "Amen" if worship is to have life. At the same time, when only one is singing or offering praise, that person stands out, draws attention, and eventually appears to be out of step. It is when praise meets praise, ascending to God as the work of the people done in common, that the glory of God descends (Ephesians 1:23). Such praise requires no effort. It is as though it is being drawn from the depth of the being, like rivers of water flowing from the belly.

In worship, we build community. The glow of one radiates toward the other. Exuberance from the uplifted one lights sparks of fire in the one toiling under the load of life. One moved upon mightily speaks as the Spirit gives utterance, and for another the burden is rolled away.

The principle that applies in worship operates in all the work we do for God. Whatever God has deposited within one member is needed for the common life and the common work. The more we understand this, the more charitable we will be to the one who has a different thought or another way of offering praise. Such building of a common life will serve us well in times of testing and trial.

But solemnity is not the only mark of our entrance to the covenant. We also enter with joy. Pondering the nature of joy can provide great insight into our life in God. On the surface the requirements of joy seem contradictory. On the one hand, joy is commanded of us; on the other hand, it is to come forth from us spontaneously.

Joy begins with the acceptance of the truth that what God says is good is indeed good. It begins with a surrender to the divine working that binds us together so the Spirit may supply true joy. God commands joy, but it is not the sort of command that comes from a tyrant or a dictator. It is more on the order of the word spoken in creation, a word that calls forth what we have been created to give, that fulfills our purpose for being. As the people of God, we are commanded, called forth to make a joyful noise, to serve the Lord with gladness, to enter God's gates with thanksgiving and God's courts with praise. This is public affirmation that we are not ashamed of one another or of the God who has joined us together (Psalm 92; 100).

As is always the case, God requires nothing of us that is not good for us. Indeed, the command of God is the best clue to what we truly need. God inhabits the praise of the worshiping people, and the presence of God brings joy. So the command to make a joyful noise is really a challenge, an opportunity. God says, "Give me glory, and I will give you joy, and with joy will come your strength" (see Nehemiah 8:10).

We can't go far in our journey without joy. Joy is like water for a desert trip. Even times of sadness, mourning, heartache, and pain give way to joy. The psalmist was correct: weeping may endure at night, but joy comes in the morning (Psalm 30:5). We draw water with joy from the well of salvation, for the joy of the Lord is our strength. As such, it is more than a feeling of exuberance or pleasure. It is not to be confused with fun or play.

True joy is rooted in our baptism. Our affections are set on things above. We experience joy from obeying and serving God. Jesus becomes the center of our joy. The closer we get to God, the more joy we receive. It's not always loud, exuberant joy but an inner satisfaction of the soul in the presence of God.

We enter joyfully into covenant because we are glad to be a part of the union into which God has brought us. This union is a source of renewal. Thus we greet one another with smiles and embraces, not with long, sad faces and spirits filled with dread.

With joy we draw from the wells of salvation, from the springs of deliverance. This joy is fruit of the Spirit, a byproduct of sin forgiven and of communion with the risen Christ in the power of the Spirit (John 4:14). Joy is to characterize our fellowship, our worship, and all we do in the name of the Lord. It is to characterize the gifts of our resources and our service. Indeed, this is one of the measures by which to know whether what we have done is unto the Lord. We frustrate joy when we seek glory, self-vindication, and a reward in this world. The glory belongs to God, but the joy belongs to us.

Joy is not to be predicated on our works. The disciples rejoiced because the demons were subject to them. They were chastised and told to rejoice because their names were written on high. For us too, rejoicing is not a result of our being worthy but that we have been counted worthy, that we have been granted fellowship with the people of God and allowed to suffer for the cause of Christ.

Solemnity and joy should not seem like opposites. Entering into covenant is serious business. But wrapped up in it is the opportunity to experience the joy that comes from praising and serving God.

➤◆◄

For Reflection and Discussion

- What words do you associate with solemnity and joy? How do these words apply to your understanding of entering into covenant?
- How is the church covenant different from covenants that involve only human relationships?
- In what ways have you experienced joy in your covenant community?

6

Walking Together in Christian Love

Lesson: Galatians 5:16-26

But if ye be led by the Spirit, ye are not under the law.
(GALATIANS 5:18)

"We engage ... by the aid of the Holy Spirit to walk together in Christian love."

Living together in Christian community is the best life one can know this side of heaven. Living as people of the Covenant exemplifies God's will being done on earth as it is in heaven. But this does not come about accidentally or automatically or by our might. To walk together in Christian love requires the aid of the Holy Spirit.

As much as we need to walk together, our tendency as humans is to walk contrary to our best interests and the interests of wholesome community. We tend to look out for number one. Invariably we define self-interest in terms of power, competition, and strategies to dominate others. This is why we need the aid of the Holy Spirit.

The concept of walking together in Christian love is consistent with what the apostle Paul meant by walking in the Spirit. In his letter to the Galatians, he admonished believers who were beset with frictions and tensions over the necessity of keeping the law to focus on their life together in Christ. The threat was so great that some were being turned from the faith, leading the apostle to conclude they had been bewitched. Indeed, the power of disharmony can be bewitching.

Only the Spirit of God can produce the Christian love that should characterize our walk with the Lord and with one another. Christian love is an antidote in a world full of hatred and insecurity. Young people who don't expect to live into their twenties need love. So do older people who have lost the ability to fully care for themselves.

The Greek word Paul uses for "walk" means to live as a companion to others. An even clearer sense of walking is offered by the word used in Galatians 5:25, where walking is the march of a military regiment in which persons are pledged to one another and to a common cause. This is intentional, purposeful walking, not just milling around or marking time. It commits a person to one direction, breaking indecision and inertia.

Walking in the Spirit is to be patterned after Christ with the power the Spirit supplies. In this walk, the law of God is fulfilled. Such a purposeful walk prevents walking after the flesh, which is utterly contrary to the will of God. Among the fruits of walking in the flesh are adultery, fornication, uncleanness, and drunkenness.

In communal life, walking after the flesh yields hatred, envy, strife, and sometimes hurtful or vengeful plots and schemes. One of the biggest mistakes believers can make is to assume we are not capable of fleshly behavior. We fool ourselves if we suppose that these tendencies apply only to "them." Anyone who is not striving to walk in Christian love by the power of the spirit can fall prey.

Paul forces us to come to terms with a view of ourselves that is consistent with the way God sees us. He insists that there is no neutral ground. The flesh and the Spirit are contrary. According to Galatians 5:17, the flesh lusts against the Spirit and the Spirit against the flesh. The powers that would destroy the works of God have no intention of relenting. We need the power of the Spirit every day and every moment.

This war against the flesh does not mean we should devalue our bodies or that we somehow reach a spiritual plane where we can serve God in detachment from the physical. In fact, the fruit of the Spirit is produced in our bodies. Love, joy, peace, long-suffering, gentleness, goodness, faith, meekness, and temperance describe ways we live in this earthly tabernacle.

The work of the Spirit within us produces positive fruit, guarding us from the works of the flesh that strive to undermine our efforts to walk together in Christian love. As we grow in grace we become keen to the strategies of the flesh. When they threaten to arise within us, we pray for a soft word to turn away wrath or seek discernment to identify those subtle forces that would turn us from the right path. We pray without ceasing, for we know the adversary is like a roaring lion, and it does not take long to be devoured (1 Peter 5:8).

But even as we lean on the power of the Holy Spirit, we must recognize that the nature of the Spirit is not to overpower us against our will. The Holy Spirit makes the power available, but we must engage it. We must open our hearts and our affairs for the Spirit to work.

My first experience in understanding what it means to engage power came when my father let me plow with a tractor instead of using a hoe. The hoe had helped me understand the limits of my power. The tractor gave me access to power beyond myself. But even with the motor running, nothing would happen until I engaged the clutch.

As believers, we are not doomed to powerless lives. There is no decree of fate that consigns our sons and daughters to prisons or to AIDS, our schools to battle zones, our communities to corruption, and our churches to confusion. Walking together in Christian love is our answer, and we access the power of love through the Holy Spirit.

Be aware, though, that when the Spirit is in control, our lives may take some unexpected turns. People we may not prefer will be brought into our lives. Our service will be summoned at inconvenient hours. These are the demands of love.

We as African American Christians have a unique opportunity to testify to love. Our ancestors were stolen from the other side of the world and brought to this land in shackles. Men and women were packed on ships like sardines and sold on the auction block like cattle. But ours is also a story of the triumph of a people who refused to let the culture's definition of them set the boundaries on their possibilities. Rather, by the help of God, we rose as evidence of God's compassion and as a sign to others that the Lord will make a way.

God calls us again today to walk together in Christian love. Our mothers and fathers were not speaking to their generation only when they cried, "Walk together, children.... The great camp meeting is not around here; it is in the Promised Land."

Walking together leaves no room for old feuds. A new generation has arisen that knows nothing of the old animosities. The needs of our communities and of the world are too great;

there is no time for petty squabbles over who gets the recognition or whose name gets called the most times. When we walk together, there are no big I's and little you's, for we are all here by the grace of God.

The Table of the Lord defies us to walk any other way. In fact, the Lord's Table stands as a judgment against a fractured community that would bring some into the inner circle and push others to the fringes. It is a judgment against those who would walk after the flesh, unclean, or who would stir up division and then come to the Table.

If we do not walk together in love, we have not discerned the Lord's body. For the bread we break is the communion of the body of Christ; the cup of blessing is the communion of the blood of Christ (Luke 22:17-20; 1 Corinthians 10:16; 11:23-26). And Christ our Passover who was slain for us is one (1 Corinthians 5:7). But if we engage by the aid of the Holy Spirit to walk together, the Table is the sign of our power. It is the promise of our victory, the seal of our joy.

ᐅᐧᐊ

For Reflection and Discussion

- In your journey of faith, what are some of the ways you engage the power of the Holy Spirit?
- Are there areas in your life where you may be coming up short when it comes to walking together in love? Are there divisions that need to be healed, opportunities to seize?
- The next time you take the bread and cup, make an effort to think about the significance of this act and its implications for unity and walking together in love.

⊒ 7 ⊑

Advancing in Knowledge and Holiness

Lesson: 2 Peter 3

But grow in grace, and in the knowledge of our Lord and Savior Jesus Christ. (2 PETER 3:18)

"We engage ... to strive for the advancement of this church in knowledge and holiness."

Striving implies a sustained effort to push beyond former boundaries. In the Covenant, the object of our striving is the advancement of the church in knowledge and holiness. In New Testament times, such a pledge was a fitting response to the direct command to believers found at the end of the second epistle of Peter. They, like we, faced the ever-present threat of becoming too comfortable, complacent, or slack as we await the consummation promised by God.

Significantly, Peter closed his epistle by enjoining believers to grow in grace, the unmerited favor of God, the gift of salvation. This suggests that the knowledge for which we strive is not knowledge in general. It is not dispassionate. Its purpose is not for the sake of debate or bragging because our attainment has exceeded another's. Rather, it is the kind of knowledge that forms us into what God called us to be. This growth in grace comes through knowledge of our Lord and Savior Jesus Christ.

Of all the ways a church can grow, to grow in knowledge and holiness stands first in line. A church may grow numerically. But it matters little if the church is not growing in its knowledge of God, its understanding of grace, and its holiness. Increase the size of a church facility without an understanding of what God has called the church to be, and members won't know what to do with their building. And so, first and foremost, we strive for greater knowledge of God.

At a basic level, this means hearing the story of God's gracious dealing with the chosen people through whom the families of the earth are to be blessed (Genesis 12:1-3). There is no substitute for rehearsing and knowing this story. In the telling and hearing of the story, we encounter the one who lays claim to our lives and who demands the obedience of faith.

We grow in knowledge through intimate, personal, and unfettered communion with the Creator. And knowledge of God comes also through understanding the Scriptures' testimony to the faithful God, who does not yield to the will of hardened oppressors and who does not relieve the chosen ones of their requirements of mercy and justice when they prosper (Micah 6:8). While our striving for knowledge begins with knowledge of God, it does not end there. We need knowledge in other areas, even in areas deemed less spiritual, in order to fulfill our calling as God's stewards.

While we appreciate the foundation laid by our mothers and fathers, we must acknowledge the partial nature of the knowledge they possessed. Their knowledge was suitable for their day. But we face circumstances they could not possibly have imagined. We confront a world that was not known to them. And so we move forward, trusting that God, who is the same yesterday, today, and forever (Hebrews 13:8), will provide an increase in knowledge sufficient for our era and for our challenges.

Thus it is essential to advance in every form of knowledge that enables our faithful service in the world. This requires mastery of the systems by which we regulate our common life. Scientific, technical, and analytic training are required if we are to be useful, and surely God intends no less. This should be pursued in service to God, and we should all take care to ensure that our pursuits in the marketplace of life do not dishonor the name of God. God does not want us to be an ignorant people.

Knowledge is not neutral. With it comes the capacity to dominate the world and to dominate others or the capacity to resist domination. As a race, African Americans have been victims of false knowledge (lies) and of lack of knowledge, from which we have sometimes been deprived. This combination has led to debilitation, to a sort of lethal impotence that in many cases is passed from one generation to the next.

In the Spirit's work of forming the persons God is seeking to make, there is an intimate connection between knowledge and holiness. Indeed, in a very real sense, holiness is the knowledge of God taking residence and transforming persons into the image of Christ. It is knowledge taking effect. Believers are made holy through the sanctifying work of the Spirit, which comes through the washing of the Word, which contains the knowledge of God. The beauty of holiness is present in the knowledge of God becoming the active ingredient in persons and communities that truly name the name of Christ.

Holiness is not a matter of choice; the choice is whether knowledge of God truly forms the life of persons and communities, or whether it remains purely formal. The choice is whether the world can look on us and see Christ, or whether the world must look over us to see Christ.

A sure remedy to half-hearted commitment is through diligent striving after knowledge of God. This means, in part, a serious study of God's Word. This must go beyond picking up the Bible on Sunday in worship or from time to time in moments of leisure. It is daily meditation and feasting on the Word that imparts the knowledge that becomes the lamp to our feet and the light to our path (Psalm 119:105). Such a commitment leaves no room for excuses for not coming to Sunday school. We need to press on Sunday like we do on Monday.

We cannot expect personal sanctification to be accomplished only on Sunday morning. It will take place when we spend time in the study of God's Word in midweek Bible studies and in special sessions.

As we strive for the advancement of the church in knowledge and holiness, let us not forget what lifted us as a people following slavery. Committed Christians devoted themselves to imparting knowledge of God and knowledge of every wholesome form to former slaves who were exiting the plantations. They built churches and later schools to impart essential knowledge that united technical and spiritual content. This allowed for the training of the mind, the heart, and the hands.

But before there were schools, the teaching took place in the churches. The same can happen today. We have the opportunity to go from our churches, find our people, and give them knowledge of God. We need to earnestly fast and pray for this missionary spirit to return.

We cannot be satisfied with a world around us starving for knowledge of God. As believers, we are to become witnesses to this knowledge. Where there is sickness, suffering, distress, or oppression no person should have to wonder about God's disposition; it should be manifest in communities that are mature in knowledge of God and holiness.

➤∎◄

For Reflection and Discussion

- What are you doing and what might you do in order to grow in your knowledge of God?
- What are some examples of knowledge being used for evil purposes and knowledge being used for good? How might the knowledge you have in a particular area be used for good?
- How can churches today have more of an influence in the world? How can your church become a source of the knowledge of God in its community?
- Discuss some ways by which knowledge of God develops personal holiness.

8

First Place in Our Affections

Lesson: Colossians 3

Set your affection on things above, not on things on the earth.... Let the word of Christ dwell in you richly in all wisdom. (COLOSSIANS 3:2,16)

"We engage ... to give [the church] a place in our affections ... above every organization of human origin."

This section of the Church Covenant addresses the question of where our affections, our priorities, our highest loyalties lie. Priorities set the tone and direction for how we live our lives. Colossians 3:2 instructs us to set our affections on things above. The affection to which this text refers is a powerful inner force that determines how personal power is dispensed. It is different from the passions within our nature that drive us to satisfy a quest for power or to indulge in pleasures that intoxicate and remove our sense for the need of God. These affections are lusts that delude us into believing that we are sufficient to ourselves or that our natural desires indicate the true nature of our need (Romans 1:26; 7:8).

In contrast, the affections to which Colossians 3:2 refers are those affections that cultivate a sensitivity to the things of Christ—a sensitivity implanted and nourished by the Spirit that produces a yearning for what God has decreed. These affections involve an inner tug that draws one by an intense longing for God's way. Thus we are dealing here with holy affections from the innermost being—a craving and hunger for God (Matthew 5:6). Thus, as members of a covenant community, we commit to give the church a place in our affections, prayers, and services above every organization of human origin. No doubt, some will wonder if the church deserves such special treatment. Is the church primarily a temporal, social institution? Or is it something more?

Many people view the church as being essentially the same as other organizations of human origin. In part the problem that gives rise to this perception is that members of the church are human beings—men and women constituted of flesh and blood. We have the evidence before our eyes that no amount of salvation terminates our humanity. The most righteous among us still possess shortcomings. For activities to proceed with any measure of smoothness there must be some degree of organization. Little observation is required to see that, in the church, tares remain among the wheat (Matthew 13:24-30). Hypocrites, backsliders, mummers, Pharisees, and persons with all sorts of faults remain in our number. We need the reminder of this Covenant! So easily the pragmatics of life in our time can corrode the strong affection the Spirit seeks to set in place. A great danger arises if we are not clear on this point: the church is not of human origin and must have the highest place in our affections.

We tend to behave in the church as if it is merely another organization or institution. For example, we sometimes make decisions concerning our commitment on purely pragmatic and essentially economic bases. Excuses we use for not attending church or becoming involved in a church function or ministry would not be good enough excuses for avoiding the workplace. Instead of receiving our best portion, the church sometimes must make do with the leftovers, the dregs of our time, energy, and passion. Thus giving the church our affection above any other human institution is quite a radical commitment.

There are strong reasons for the church being worthy of our highest affection. Unlike other institutions, the church was instituted by our Lord. Its origin is in the will of the Father, the sacrifice of the Son, and the power of the Spirit. Apart from this accounting, perhaps it would deserve no greater attention than any other organization. But Jesus declared, "Upon this rock I will build my church; and the gates of hell shall not prevail against it" (Matthew 16:18).

Repeatedly in the epistles the church is called the body of Christ. The Spirit brings believers to a fuller realization and appreciation of the church as a holy institution. Short of this insight, believers become lackadaisical toward it, and nonbelievers come to resent it. After all, the church has no legitimacy without this special dimension that sets it apart. It has no right to make the claims it does, to take up the space it occupies, to demand the resources required unless it is special, ordained to carry out the purposes of God. Indeed, the church is the primary channel God has chosen through which grace is given to the world.

By means of the church the gospel of salvation is to reach the world, the light is to be spread to the nations, healing is to be supplied to the land, the glory of God is to be revealed, and witness to the coming kingdom is to be made. To be sure, the church is not valuable and precious because of our affections. Rather, it deserves our affections because it is inherently precious and valuable. Just as God gave grace to the world through the embodiment of the Son, Jesus Christ, so God's love for the world remains in the tangible sign—the church. In granting the church our affections, we must be careful not to love it wrongly or treat it selfishly, as if it is our possession. For ultimately it is not the church we love but the God to whom we are drawn through the church.

Covenanting to put no organization above the church is a simple, direct, straightforward vow. Nothing is to be equal to or rival the church when it comes to commitment and loyalty. The best of our resources, time, talent, and attention is not to be given to some other cause or organization.

Initially this phrase in the Covenant was intended to address the issue of membership in organizations that unduly influenced the decisions of those possessing authority within the church—in other words, secret orders. But the application is not solely to the lodge. It could even apply to clubs within the church or to attachment to traditions that are in conflict with the church God is calling forth.

Our affections are determined not by what we say with our lips but through what we do with our hands, our time, our energy. Such commitment is visible, tangible, empirical, observable by others. Giving the church its proper place in our affections entails praying for the church, giving it our service, becoming involved in its ministries, being drawn into the church's life through the communion of the Spirit. It is touching and being touched by its purposes. This does not mean that we should neglect our families and other social responsibilities. In fact, fulfilling these other responsibilities is part of our calling as members of a covenant community. Our faith is to guide everything we do. Our affection for God is to regulate our behavior in our homes, on our jobs, everywhere we go. Wherever we are, the vitality of the church is to be present, and the joy resulting from the Spirit working in us is to energize the people of God when we reassemble.

Finally, we give first place to the church because through the church God gives the grace of life. We begin a week by coming together to worship the risen Christ, thereby receiving grace and power for the journey of another week. We give of our time and resources because in strengthening the church we lend strength to the body through which we are sustained and through which God accomplishes the purposes of healing, blessing, and salvation.

⁊⹁⹁

For Reflection and Discussion

- Why should the church be set apart from other institutions, even those with similar missions?
- What gives the church the greatest competition for the affections of people you know? What about for you?
- What can you do to show your affection for the church of God? What about your local church?

⊒ 9 ⊑

Sustain Worship

Lesson: Psalms 95–96

Let the word of Christ dwell in you richly in all wisdom; teaching and admonishing one another in psalms and hymns and spiritual songs, singing with grace in your hearts to the Lord. And whatsoever you do in word or deed, do all in the name of the Lord Jesus, giving thanks to God and the Father by him. (COLOSSIANS 3:16-17)

"We engage ... to sustain [the church's] worship, ordinances, discipline and doctrine."

For the church's life to be vital and vibrant takes committed persons who are deeply devoted to God. The alternative to vitality and vibrancy is a church that is moribund, static, stale. It draws nobody. The Covenant calls us—and nobody else—to sustain the church's worship. Without question, worship is the heartbeat of the church.

Above all else, the church is a worshiping community. It is the opportunity for those who know their end in life to give glory to the Father and adoration to the Son Jesus Christ in the power of the Spirit. The soul finds fulfillment and completion in the presence of the Lord.

Worship lifts us by the might of the Spirit into the heavenly places where we can be still before God. It keeps us from being riveted to mundane things that prevent the spirit from soaring (Ephesians 2:16). In worship we find the refreshment that comes from the Lord. As the psalmist said, in God's presence there is fullness of joy, and at God's right hand there are pleasures for evermore (Psalm 16:11). Nothing else the believer does can be compared with the worship of God.

Worship is like the breath of the body entering and going forth. It keeps the church alive. Through prayer the church is connected to the source of its power. Through praise there is ascension to God. Through the singing of songs the heart is made glad. Through the preaching and teaching of the Word the church is sanctified. Where there is no vitality in worship within a Christian community, there will be vitality in nothing else.

However, true vitality in worship can be a foundation for other activities pleasing to God. True worship is in Spirit and truth, which is to say that it is not the form of worship that matters but the substance. As our mothers and fathers in the faith put it, "We did not come for form or fashion, or for outside show to the world. But we come like empty pitchers before a full fountain desiring to be filled." Jesus told the woman at the well the issue was not whether the worship took place on Mount Zion or Mount Gerizim. What mattered was that it be in Spirit and in truth (John 4:22-23).

To sustain vital worship, members of the community must be present in body and in spirit. Repeatedly the psalmist invited the people of God to worship, to bow down before God, to sing, and to offer praises. The invitation to worship is to leave whatever else preoccupies the mind and to gather in the presence of the Lord. This is not to say there is no personal and private devotion wherein the believer comes before the Lord in supplication, intercession, and refreshment. But nothing takes the place of worship as the ingathering of God's people.

Worship is God saying with authority that by far exceeds that of the sternest parent, "Come here!" For a space of time we are called from any form of isolation or other engagement to stand with others. In the presence of God and joined with one another, we are to bow down, to sing, to clap our hands, to be joyful, and to hear from God. In true worship we join with all creation, the host of heaven, and the saints who have preceded us in giving glory to God.

Worship entails joining with others by a release of the self through the Spirit. Worship is not something that is done for us. It is not a performance or entertainment, where some are paid to do the job for others. It is not like a show, where professionals offer their talent while the paying audience sits back watching and critiquing. Rather, to worship is to be involved, to participate, and to enter fully and freely into an offering that is going forth to God. True worship brings persons into the presence of God and into the lives of one another in a manner marked by what the Spirit gives and sustains—namely, unity, communion, fellowship.

The trajectory of worship is upward. With reverence and awe, we come into the presence of God. We don't presume to come into God's presence in just any sort of way. Worship time is hallowed time. It is not time to catch up on the latest gossip, to watch what others are wearing, or to worry about who is watching us. It is time to turn aside from all that preoccupies us, to put all petty issues aside and accept God's priorities. If we bring burdens to worship, we do so for the purpose of laying them down. But we come mainly to glorify the name of the Lord and to be built up in faith.

"O come, let us sing unto the LORD: let us make a joyful noise to the rock of our salvation," says the psalmist (Psalm 95:1). It is a beckoning to what those being invited should recognize as good. There is excitement and consensus that it is right to make a joyful noise, for the praise is directed to the rock of salvation. There is acknowledgment that all blessings have been given by God. And the proper response is to bow down, to kneel before the Lord our maker.

In its root, worship signifies bowing, bending the body, showing reverence. The worshiper in Old Testament times often lay prostrate, with the face to the ground and the body fully extended. This showed absolute, unreserved reverence in full acknowledgment of the source of authority and power. Bodily motions of crouching and falling down made it clear that no insurrection or challenge of any sort was being offered. In ancient times this was the manner in which rulers were approached. But we show such reverence only to God.

Psalm 96:9 continues with an invitation to "worship the LORD in the beauty of holiness: fear before him, all the earth." Worshiping in the beauty of holiness entails offering one's self to God for beautification. We bring ourselves into the divine presence so the holiness of God can permeate our beings and beauty can be reflected in us. This beautification removes the ugliness of sin and rebellion.

This is accomplished in part through the ordinances, disciplines, and doctrines, all of which restore the image of God in the Son by the Spirit's power. Indeed, this dimension of our corporate life must not be divorced from our worship, as it affects worship decisively. We cannot be negligent in these matters and expect worship to be in Spirit and truth.

The ordinances—baptism and the Lord's Supper—constitute the highest expression of our worship. In a sense, every gathering is a celebration of our baptism and a remembrance of the body and blood of Christ. The occasion for worship is that we have been buried with Christ in baptism and raised with him to walk in newness of life (Romans 6:4). We are no longer abandoned in a world that is perishing, but we have been brought into the ark of safety, into a zone of protection from the storms of life (Matthew 20:18-29; 1 Peter 3:20-21).

The reading, preaching, and teaching of the Word constitute the connection between these ordinances and authentic worship. The reading and hearing of the Word enable us to hear what God says to us. In the teaching of the Word we are given the knowledge of God that forms disciples. In preaching, the living Word is among us as God addresses the people through a human vessel in ways that compel a response.

We cannot separate worship from our lives outside of church, for worship is a gathering of disciples who live under the saving influences of the Spirit and the rule of Christ. We don't live just any sort of way and then come to worship. In response to the Word, we have made an agreement concerning how we will live. There is a sense in which we return in worship to report victory or to gain needed strength for our walk with the Lord. The hymn writer Isaac Watts was not amiss in enjoining: "Let those refuse to sing who never knew our God; but children of the heavenly king may speak their joys abroad." And our Lord has instructed those with anything against a brother or a sister to leave their gift at the altar, to make things right, and then go to worship (Matthew 5:23-24).

It cannot be emphasized enough that worship is to be guided by the doctrine of Christ. We are not to speak errors when we worship, and we must not be offended when we are corrected. Those who lead, teach, sing, and preach must be careful not to misspeak in the utterance that goes forth. True worship of God must be anchored in sound doctrine (1 Timothy 1:6-11).

Worship in the early church was patterned primarily after the Jewish synagogue. In the early church, temple worship was not available to most of the people. Only during feast times could those in the scattered places behold the pageantry and see the beauty of worship as the sacrifice was offered and the smoke and incense went up to God. Temple worship, epitomized in the sacrifice, was fulfilled in Christ, who is the priest and the offering. As the people of the new covenant, we offer the sacrifice of thanksgiving and praise (1 Peter 2:5).

In Ephesians 5:19 we are told that our worship is an overflow of the life that is filled with the Spirit. In that overflow we are to sing psalms, hymns, and spiritual songs, making melody in our hearts, giving thanks to the Father in the name of our Lord Jesus Christ. The instruction of Colossians commands us to let the word of Christ dwell in us richly, for thereby we are taught how to worship—in psalms, hymns, and spiritual songs, singing with grace in our hearts to the Lord (Colossians 3:16).

In a profound sense, all we do as God's people is to be done with an attitude of worship. Discipline and doctrine are to be dispensed with an attitude of worship. The order of worship may change, but Bible study, choir rehearsal, even committee meetings and conferences should be done in an atmosphere of worship, for we are not dealing merely with formal principles and agenda items but with how our personal lives and our common life are to reflect and radiate the beauty of the Lord our God.

Worship is given to enliven and invigorate the church. We are to make a "joyful noise." This is not to say there is never a time for solemnity or blessed quietness. Neither is it to say that joyful noise is the same as frivolity, mirth, or bringing a partying spirit into the church. But we serve the true and living God, and worship is not somber and sad. Even funerals for the saint of God are to be joyful.

We sustain the church's worship when we accept this unsurpassed invitation: "Make a joyful noise unto the LORD, all ye lands. Serve the LORD with gladness: come before his presence with singing.... Enter into his gates with thanksgiving.... For the LORD is good..." (Psalm 100:1-2,4-5).

➤∎◀

For Reflection and Discussion

- In what way is a church's vitality and ministry influenced by the vitality of its worship?
- What principles distinguish worship as glorifying God from worship as a performance?
- What are some common differences between our purposes in worship and God's priorities?
- Is it possible for worship to be genuine if there is no substance or if the substance is misguided? Why or why not?

10

Contribute Cheerfully and Regularly

Lessons: Proverbs 3:9; Malachi 3:10; Matthew 23:23; 2 Corinthians 8–9

Each man should give what he has decided in his heart to give, not reluctantly or under compulsion, for God loves a cheerful giver. (2 CORINTHIANS 9:7, NIV)

✶

"Contribute cheerfully and regularly ... for the support of a faithful and evangelical ministry among us, the relief of the poor and the spread of the gospel throughout the world."

Why do Christians give? Is it so church members can brag about their fine building and keep their preacher well dressed? Is it so treasurers can report positive balances? Unfortunately these are among the thoughts of people inside and outside the church. Such thinking is opposite the biblical concept of giving as a joy and a grace. In fact, the Spirit enables believers to give not grudgingly or of necessity but cheerfully.

There is no way to be a follower of Christ without giving. God is a giving God. The Father gave the Son that whosoever believeth in him should not perish (John 3:16). The Son gave his life as a perfect sacrifice to purge our consciences from dead works to serve the living God. The Spirit is given as the power of life who gives us the grace to obey and please God.

A proper attitude toward giving begins with the recognition that we are not proprietors but stewards. We brought nothing into this world, and it is certain that we will carry nothing out. None of us has anything that was not given to us. Beginning with our life, all comes from God—the air we breathe, the water we drink, the space we occupy. Even the strength with which we might resist the divine command comes from the Creator. How quickly we can lose all we think we have! In a moment, in the twinkling of an eye, the ground opens, the winds swirl, the side of the mountain slides, the car crashes, the plane falls. Then where do the possessions go?

Why do we give unto the Lord? The pragmatic reason that easily comes to our lips is so the work of the Lord can be sustained. This is the reason stated in the Covenant. But more is at stake in giving, for giving is an attitude of the heart, an orientation of the affection, an outpouring of the self. Jesus put it this way: "Where you treasure is, there will your heart be also" (Matthew 6:21). Our giving signifies what we cherish; it establishes the priorities for our life. In this sense, giving is a discipline of the Spirit that orders our steps.

The pattern for Christian giving was set under the old covenant as a form of worship. Abraham offered a tithe to Melchizedek upon his return from the battle in which he rescued Lot and his company. Upon encountering this priest of God, Abraham expressed his gratitude that God prevailed and the life of his nephew was not lost (Genesis 14:20). Repeatedly the tithe is in the law and the instructions to the people as acknowledgment of their dependence on God and their gratitude for the blessing bestowed upon them.

The tithe is one-tenth, but not just any one-tenth. It was the first portion, the first fruits that the land yielded, not the leftovers. The tithe brought to the temple and stored in the chambers was for the priests and Levites to be sustained and so the work of the temple could proceed. Also, in the storehouse of the Lord provisions were to be made for the poor, the destitute, and the stranger.

The people were taught that the tithe belonged to God. Hence withholding it was an act of robbing God, and it put them in line to receive the Lord's judgment. Giving the tithe was an act of consecration for the portion remaining, and the promise was that nine parts receiving divine blessing amount to more than all ten parts without the blessing (Leviticus 27:30-34).

God promised in return for the tithe that the windows of heaven would be opened; blessings that cannot be measured would be outpoured. But withholding the tithe would yield a consequence described by the image of divine breath that comes like a scattering wind (Malachi 3:8-10).

All sorts of questions arise surrounding the tithe. Do I pay on the gross or the net? Do I pay it all at once or week by week? Should I designate where the portions go? Do I still pay an offering? Suppose I pay tithes and find myself unable to meet other obligations? Perhaps the most pointed question of all is whether the tithe was done away with under the new covenant. These are not frivolous questions, and there probably isn't anyone who has not asked them at one time or another.

A response to these questions must begin with the assertion that tithing, in the old and the new covenants, is first and foremost a form of worship. Giving the tithe honors God with the first fruits. The ancient people of God did not know the system of taxation with which we live. Gross or net would have made no sense to them. To focus on such a question, however, takes us into excessive legalism. Suffice it to say that if you tithe on what comes into your hand, you will do well. But if you have already experienced the grace that comes from doing more, there is no power sufficient to make you change. Furthermore, whether you give by the week or give by the month, what matters is whether you are doing it as unto the Lord.

After paying tithes can you still meet your obligations? I suggest soliciting testimony from tithers! Remember that tithing is an act of faith. Each person must be satisfied in his or her mind.

Is tithing a carryover into the New Testament church? Jesus gives the best answer to this in his excoriation of the Pharisees. They turned tithing, like every other provision of the law, into legalism. That is, they kept the law as a badge of piety to put on display and distinguish them from others whom they considered sinners. They honored God with their lips and other overt acts, but their hearts were not in what they did. Speaking specifically of the tithe, Jesus said they gave as a substitute for observing the weightier matters—like mercy, justice, and faith. Jesus' response was that the tithe should be given and the other not neglected (Matthew 23:23).

Giving to the Lord as a tangible, concrete aspect of our life in God is not to be separated from other acts of devotion and consecration. Giving is a spiritual act. Done for the glory of

God, it draws us more fully into the will of God and brings us more closely to the place where God can truly use us.

The practical results of the spiritual act support the ministries and needs of the covenant community. When a need arises, the church should not have to scramble to meet it. Lack of financial resources should not detract from its primary work of glorifying God and blessing the world. Like a mighty army poised for battle, the church should be ready to face any foe and meet every challenge. The grace of giving enables it to do so.

Our obedience should not be based on how much we say we can afford. Spiritually speaking, this thinking is backwards. Rather, God wants us to give first, not in a grudging or calculating manner but to build a bounty to be on hand for when the need arises.

This differs from the way many of us think about our stewardship, especially in a debt-driven economy. Most of us, myself included, do all within our power not to keep up but to keep from getting further behind. This is not because we lack but because we are already partaking of too much of the bounty. Some decisions related to how we use our resources have been made for us by the culture concerning how we ought to live, and unless we are extremely careful, we ratify them without taking notice. The number of suits, shoes, or dresses (our wants) tend to have more to do with the way we see ourselves in our social setting than with what we need. The instruction to the church is to put the bounty up front. The church of God should never get caught with the beggar's cup. Rather, it should have bounty with which to bless those of its number who are in need, as well as to bless the world.

Blessing the world entails being faithful and evangelical. We are heralds of the good news that God has given salvation to the world. The power of sin has been broken, and God has inaugurated the first phase of the kingdom within the church. The church is the place where those seeking salvation from the raging storm of life are to be welcomed. It is an ark of safety, a tower of refuge, a land like Goshen that has been spared the plague that comes from the judgment of God. It is wonderful when those who already know the Lord come to cast their lot among us. But our first duty in ministry is to rescue the perishing who are around us.

Evangelical ministry requires bounty. It ought not first calculate what the weary ones can bring. The target group is not set based on salary, class, race, income, or any other variable that predicts desirability. Evangelical ministry is patterned after the invitation of the Lord, who cried, "Come unto me, all ye that labor and are heavy laden, and I will give you rest" (Matthew 11:28). It requires a bounty on hand, as seen in the actions of the Lord, who would not permit the disciples to send the multitude away for food (Matthew 14:15-16).

We must stand against the thinking that would drive a wedge between evangelical and social ministry. Many people have latched onto the shibboleth "saving souls" as though this is something unrelated to the condition in which people live and the obstacles they must face even after embracing new life in Christ. Evangelical ministry requires us to demonstrate that the same Jesus who died for our sins is a Savior who is filled with compassion. The one who calls us out of darkness and wills that none should perish desires that we live productive lives. Indeed, it is God's will for those who are comforted to receive sufficient vitality to return to others the comfort they have received (2 Corinthians 1:3-4).

A truly evangelical word for this day is one that gives hope in the face of the crisis and the storms of life. It is not to be confused with the approach that blames all people's problems on social or genetic factors, rendering them helpless victims. Nor is it to pretend there are not forces that favor some and hurt others. Rather, it is a word that provides a vision of God breaking into the bleakest circumstances, empowering men and women to rise from the dung heap and claim their God-given destiny.

While the primary purpose is to bring men and women into the fold, some resources must go to meet human need without regard to personal faith. And some must go toward the spread of the gospel in places where we will never go. In this way we acknowledge and participate in the sacrifice of those who have given up everything to follow Christ. This is our partnership with those who have heeded the call to go into all the world and preach the gospel (Matthew 28:19-20).

In all our giving and in all it accomplishes, let us never forget that in giving we are responding to what has been given to us. May each act of giving remind us that somebody sent by God labored for our salvation and nurture, and God is counting on us to be channels through which this marvelous grace can continue to flow.

⌖

For Reflection and Discussion

- List several motivations for giving. List them in order of importance, based on God's priorities.
- What testimony have you heard from tithers? Amplify the distinction between a proprietor and a steward.
- How have you experienced the joy of giving?
- Describe the relationship between giving and a church's vitality.

⊒ 11 ⊑

Avoid a Contentious Spirit

Lesson: Romans 12:6-21

If it be possible, as much as lieth in you, live peaceably with all [people]. (ROMANS 12:18)

"*In case of difference of opinion in the church, we will strive to avoid a contentious spirit, and if we cannot unanimously agree, we will cheerfully recognize the right of the majority to govern.*"

Getting along with one another can be hard. In fact, it may well be the greatest challenge of the church. In one sense, it seems odd that this should be so difficult. After all, we don't feel any better when we are not getting along. And obviously not getting along does not bring more glory to God—all the high and lofty confessions concerning who we are in Christ can effectively be nullified for failure to get along in the church.

Getting along is a fairly straightforward admonition. But it is far more easily said than done. So often we get tripped up by focusing on who had the last word, who didn't shake my hand, who looked at me funny, what he or she said about me. We overinterpret a tone of voice or an expression on the face. A retort may be justified but should be restrained. Getting along requires constant attention. As with other matters, we need the aid of the Spirit.

The high calling of God in Christ Jesus beckons us beyond the protocol of our culture. Our communion with Christ enjoins us to bear one another's burdens, to seek the good of all, to speak with one voice by the Spirit's aid (Galatians 6:2).

We find in Acts 15 a sort of case study focusing on how some deeply divided followers of Christ learned to get along. The struggle concerned whether Gentiles should be converted to Judaism and circumcised before being brought into the church. The Judaizers insisted that circumcision come first; Paul and his company insisted that faith in Jesus as Messiah took precedence over any keeping of the law. This issue threatened to wreck the young church. So what did they do? They spent time in prayer and fasting, waiting to hear from the Lord. The solution was one that was mutually acceptable: only the requirements essential to faith were imposed on Gentiles. Paul and those who opposed insisting on circumcision were sent to the Gentiles, while those who preferred circumcision were sent to the Jews. They accounted for the answer they received, saying, "It seemed good to the Holy Ghost and to us" (Acts 15:28).

Paul applied this pattern in response to the question of eating meat offered to idols (1 Corinthians 8). He knew that since the idol has no reality, it is incapable of causing harm. However, callousness on the part of the strong members of the community could do injury to the conscience of the weaker ones.

Paul operated based on the priority of the church being one body and members of one another. We are called to be of one mind. We are to live peaceably with one another. God means for us to get along with one another, and this we covenant to do.

That said, differences of opinion should not surprise us. But first, let's be clear we are not talking about opinions of every sort. In matters of doctrine, there is only one right opinion (orthodoxy), which is not subject to referendum. We do not vote on whether we believe in God who is Father, Son, and Holy Spirit. We may vote on who the pastor and the deacons will be, but we do not vote on whether to have a pastor and deacons. We act similarly in other matters where we are under the rule of Scripture, ordinances, discipline, and doctrine.

Beyond issues of orthodoxy, the Covenant assumes there will be differences of opinion. There is nothing inherently wrong with differences. But amid these differences, we are to strive to avoid a contentious spirit.

We have experienced a contentious spirit, perhaps even in ourselves at times. A contentious spirit is ornery, cantankerous, unresponsive to the Word of God, to sound reasoning, or to the counseling and remonstration of others. It is manifest in one who gets the head set in a given direction and refuses to be persuaded of any other point of view. Often it grows out of strong convictions and good intentions, but it is defined by its refusal to be subject to the influence of others.

The premise underlying this portion of the Covenant is that each of us can be taught something. None of us has all the insight, all the wisdom, all the understanding. Indeed, there is knowledge that we will achieve only when the mist has rolled away and we come fully into the presence of the Lord (1 Corinthians 13:12). And so we are called to humility.

The contentious spirit leaves an opening for the Enemy. Indeed, this is often the route the Enemy takes to enter the church. The contentious spirit is exceedingly deceitful in that so often it puts opposition among those who truly love one another. In family feuds and church fights, notice how the most ardent opponents are people who were close to one another at one time. The most vicious fights are often among those among whom there was once a bond forged in love. Bonds forged in love are not made to be broken. Given the seamlessness of love, there is no place for a neat separation. The rupture can only be jagged, ragged, and vicious. Thus it is incumbent upon those who would live peaceably to know the difference between expressing a legitimate difference of opinion and manifesting a contentious spirit.

In the midst of differences of opinion, we strive for the goal of unanimous agreement, a worthy goal for all the church's departments, auxiliaries, and committees. We must stand against the idea that such a goal is not realistic, for we are striving for this achievement by the aid of the Holy Spirit, the author of unity. Remember how the Spirit was given on the Day of Pentecost: reversing the curse of Babel, breaking down the barriers to worshiping God in Spirit and in truth, and establishing communion with brothers and sisters, who, like us, have been baptized into Christ's death and resurrection (Acts 2:7-12).

Reaching unanimous agreement does not mean that differences of opinion will disappear. Nor does it mean that a dissent is necessarily a sign of being contrary or contentious. Some minority opinions eventually win the day. In any case, we should not assume all opposition is motivated by evil intent.

Seeking unanimous agreement requires taking into consideration the multitude of opinions that may be present within a group of persons concerned. In this process, every person counts and every opinion matters. This applies to longtime members, as well as to newcomers and even children. And we should steer clear of moves to divide the house and rush to a vote. Rushing to a vote before all have the chance to be heard will not address the truly serious issues within the church but will only deepen the division.

Godly rule within the church comes with the spiritual gift of *kubenesis*, referred to in Romans 12:8 as "ruling" and 1 Corinthians 12:28 as "government" or "administration." This is not the pattern that operates in corporate America. It is not the same as the parliamentary moves we see in politics. Rather, the process is governed by the grace and guidance of the Holy Spirit. It is thoroughly saturated with charity, love that suffers long. It calls for behavior that is kind, not easily provoked. There is no room in this approach for the kind of memory that holds a grudge perpetually and waits for the opportunity to return the indignity previously suffered. This way of living together takes at face value the claim that we are all members of one body.

With suffering, violence, and desperation on the rise in the world, the only one getting joy out of church splits and fights is the devil. Fights bring no joy to those who lose; they leave no enduring joy to those who win. Everyone walks away from this form of spiritual warfare wounded, limping like Jacob. What's more, fights disappoint those who have come to church for refuge from the storms of life. Understandably, new converts wonder what they have got themselves into.

The godly way to resolve conflict is to reason and pray with those whose opinions differ from ours, seeking to achieve common ground. This common ground in all likelihood will not favor any particular opinion totally. Rather, it will reflect the love and care members of the Body have for one another.

In the midst of differing opinions, we commit to accept the opinion of the majority. We do so respecting the ideas and motives of those with whom we disagree. There are no winners or losers, for what we have in common remains greater than what has divided us.

God is calling the church to get along in a manner that prepares citizens for heaven. Indeed, our life in Christ is to be a foretaste of glory divine. The more we experience this foretaste, the more successful we will be in modeling the kingdom of God to the world.

＞.＜

For Reflection and Discussion

- What are some signs of a contentious spirit? Do you recognize any of these signs in your life?
- Discuss some disputes you are aware of that got out of hand. How could this have been prevented?
- List and discuss some good principles for resolving disputes in the church.
- Is it harder for you to be a gracious winner or a good loser? Why is that and how do you seek to change that failing?
- Describe a situation in which a winner may actually be the loser.

12

Maintain Devotion

Lessons: Leviticus 6:13; Matthew 6:1-15;
Deuteronomy 6; Psalm 119

"And when you pray, do not be like the hypocrites, for they love to pray ... to be seen by men.... But when you pray, go into your room, close the door and pray to your Father, who is unseen. Then your Father, who sees what is done in secret, will reward you." (MATTHEW 6:5-6, NIV)

"We also engage to maintain family and secret devotion."

The good confession of faith that Jesus is our Lord can easily be reduced to mere words and empty intentions. So much claims our attention; so many activities fill our days. Work and leisure can prove to be distractions if we do not give form to our faith. Yet faith must not be reduced to mere form, for while form forces a degree of regularity and consistency, the Spirit assures the intensity, vitality, and fire. Devotion unites form with fire as the means by which we remain in communion with God.

Our daily and constant devotion keeps the fires of our faith burning strong. Going from one Sunday to the next is not enough. Too many things can take place in that time span. Too many hard knocks can come to throw us to the ground. Too much criticism can be directed our way, reaching us like cold water to douse the flame. Practicing our faith is not confined to Sunday mornings. Day by day, hour by hour, moment by moment, the embers of the fire need to come our way. It is the will of God that the fire continues to burn on the altars of our hearts. At any moment we may be confronted with the challenge for which communion with God is the only source of our strength.

We maintain family devotion because the entire household of believers is claimed by God. This is the reason we dedicate children to the Lord. In fact, every so often we should remind our children that they were given to God.

Believers are not to despise an unbelieving spouse but should instead trust the Lord, who promises that he or she will be drawn by the godly influence (1 Corinthians 7:14; 1 Peter 3:1-2). Unbelieving spouses belong to God even if they have not yet made the good confession of faith.

The atmosphere that prevails in the church begins in the home. If there is no devotion (fire) in the home, there will be little in the church. There should be some time in a godly home where everyone who abides therein is brought into one place at one time into the presence of God.

Devotion is the activity that sets the tone for our day, for our life, for the way we use our time, energy, and talents. It reveals that to which we are devoted, given, driven with a singleness of heart and determination of the mind. Devotion, which includes learning to pray and teaching our children to pray, is the secret to overcoming the barriers that seek to impede and hinder.

Teaching the family to pray is one of the greatest gifts we can give our children. Prayer in the schools has been turned into a political issue, about which there are legitimate differences of opinion. Suffice it to say that it is ironic that we would attempt to control a sphere over which we do not have authority if we do not control the sphere that has been given to us. We cannot expect children to learn to pray at school. But the church, and families within the church, can and should claim this responsibility.

The Covenant enjoins church members to maintain a time of devotion—in their homes—with their children. In the home is where the tone is set. Devotion is to the spiritual dimension of the home what the thermostat is to the physical environment. Around the table and in many other informal family settings is where the meaning of life is taught and values are instilled. The home is where children are taught to fear God, to give and receive respect, to set goals, to learn the value of work and perseverance.

This is not solely a matter of direct, formal instruction but has to do with the environment in which children are nurtured. Formal reading of the Scriptures or reciting prayers is not necessarily enough. After all, it is possible to rush through the Lord's Prayer as a formal exercise and then go from there to activities diametrically opposed to the will of God.

A home in which sincere devotion to God is the normative and permeating influence will not promote or bear contrary behavior. The climate will forbid certain activities and attitudes. The terms for what is permitted and what is not permitted in the home are clearly set when there is devotion to God. By contrast, there is space for evil to enter when devotion to God is not prominently kept in the fore.

The Covenant speaks also of secret devotion. Jesus said we

are to go into the secret closet, and when we have shut the door we are to pray to the Father who sees in secret. And the Father who sees in secret will reward us openly. Here we have the counterpart to public devotion. One could almost conclude that Jesus set a priority on the secret devotion. This ran counter to the hypocrisy of the Pharisees, who loved to put their piety on display. Jesus was clear in telling them they had already received their reward (Matthew 6).

Secret devotion consists of unimpeded communion with the Lord. Here we can tell the Lord all about our troubles, our frustration, our anxiety, without concern over what others will think or how someone might take advantage for knowing our weakness. When calling on the Lord, we need not worry about getting a busy signal or being upbraided for the number of times we call. Secret devotion is where we have God all to ourselves. As our mothers and fathers put it, "There are days I'd like to be all alone with Christ my Lord; I can tell him all my troubles all alone."

The spiritual discipline of maintaining devotion is indispensable for a rich and productive life. Some people might say they haven't got the time for this. But this reveals a lack of knowledge concerning how the power and vitality of life truly flow. This discipline does not so much take time; rather, it makes time. For time spent in devotion is returned several-fold in the course of a single day. The centeredness, the focus, the cure for drifting, the engagement of the tasks of a day more than repay the investment of these moments spent with the Lord.

An on-again, off-again approach will not work for those who would be on fire for the Lord. It may suffice for certain formal presentations of religiosity. It may do for an hour on Sunday morning of liturgically correct ceremony. For some this is what religion is, and for them it is satisfactory. But a church that has only this sort of religion cannot grow. Maintaining devotion is not merely about doing what is proper but about tapping into God's power.

Your secret closet can be wherever you make it or wherever you take it. Wherever it is, it is a special place—holy ground that is sectioned off from the rest of the world. It is a place of quiet rest, a place where sin cannot molest—as the hymn goes—near to the heart of God. It might be the side of the bed early in the morning before anything else in the house stirs. Some who stay on the move must find that secret closet being the wheel of the automobile during a long commute. Others might find it during a break when they steal away from co-workers. But wherever it is, it keeps the fire burning on the altar of the heart.

According to the Lord, the closet may be secret, but not the reward. The reward comes in the open. That is, the benefits of this devotion will be plain and visible. Devoting the home to God pays off in an environment that is loving and affirming. Children are well behaved, or they can be constrained when they need to be brought back in line.

Most of all, the retreat to the secret closet is manifest in the blessedness of a life where the fire is kept burning. The Lord orders the footsteps so they can be steady even in the storms. The Spirit fills the mouth with the word fitly spoken while others in the same situation may sin with the tongue (Proverbs 25:11). In the trials and tragedies of life, there is confidence that though walking through the valley of the shadow of death, there is no need to fear evil (Psalm 23:4). And from time to time, the one who gives the fire and meets us in the secret closet will allow for an overflow of blessing that all can see. It may be material or spiritual, but it comes with an abundance that causes others to take notice and affords the occasion for thanksgiving.

➤∎◄

For Reflection and Discussion

- In what ways have you experienced (or heard testified) family devotion making a positive difference in the life of children and the family?
- Where is your secret closet? What time of day is most suitable for your devotion? And how do you protect that time?

⊒ 13 ⊑

Study Diligently

Lessons: Matthew 21:1-15; Zechariah 9

Thy word have I hid in mine heart, that I might not sin against thee.... Thy word is a lamp unto my feet, and a light unto my path.... The entrance of thy words giveth light; it giveth understanding unto the simple. (PSALM 119:11,105,130)

"We also engage ... to study diligently the word of God; to religiously educate our children."

In Hebrew the term for "word" is *dabar*. *Dabar* implies not just a string of letters arranged in a certain pattern and possessing a fixed meaning. It implies breath, life. It carries a connotation of mediating the power of the one who spoke the word.

With the word—*dabar*—came the power to perform. And for that reason it could not be retracted. Remember how Esau desired his father to retract the blessing given to Jacob following the scheme? Isaac could not comply, because his word—his irretrievable word—could not be drawn back. This is the understanding of those who sought to withstand Amos: they enjoined him to flee, knowing the land was not able to contain his words. The prophet Isaiah, speaking as an oracle of God, declared that God's word would not return void. It would accomplish what it was sent to perform.

The Word of God is God-breathed, inspired by the Spirit. It cannot be reduced to mere alphabet and print. As Peter put it, holy men of old were moved upon by the Holy Ghost to produce the autographs that are alive with vitality by the Spirit (2 Peter 1:21).

The psalmist of Israel says of the Word that it has gone out into all the world, and like the sun, nothing is hid from its rays. Its entrance gives light and understanding; it gives knowledge to those who are simple. The Word is a lamp to the feet and a light to the path. When hidden in the heart it prevents sin. Taking heed to it will cleanse a young person from sinful ways. Meditating, studying, chewing—it makes one see that the Lord is good, for his Word is sweeter than honey in the comb.

This psalmist, so deeply in love with the Word, provides clues for what it means to study the Word. To study the Word means to be moved upon, illumined by the same Spirit through whom we received the Word. The Word is the living, vibrating, healing, comforting presence of God, who speaks to us in blessed communion.

We see that there is a difference between a collection of words and the Word. The Bible is not an ornament to be laid around the house for decoration, to keep at least one spot on the table from catching dust. It is more than a present to be given at graduation or when we cannot think of anything else to give. The Bible is not mere decoration for the back of the pews of the church. It is the treasure of the church and the personal treasure of every believer.

In part, the beauty of what we covenant here is the underlying assumption that every believer has access to the Scriptures. This should not be taken for granted. For centuries the Scriptures were the possession of the priests and the doctors of the church. Scrolls copied by hand were not available to the masses. Neither were the people to be trusted with the reading or handling of the sacred writ. The faithful were read to in the sacred language—whether Greek or Latin—no matter what language they spoke and understood. The priest gave them what they were supposed to know.

The attitude many people still have toward the Word is that it is for the pastor, the deacons, and the teachers to read, and they in turn dispense the meaning. This is true up to a point: there is a faithful dispensation of the Word entrusted to those with guardianship for the souls of the people. But that is not the whole story; we believe that all believers are permitted—indeed, instructed by God—to read the Word for themselves. What's more, knowledge is given by the Spirit so the Word that is read will come to life with vitality and power.

We study the Word in part to understand our true identity in God's eyes. Without the truth of the Word, we are subject to being told anything by those who do not love us and who seek to dominate us. We know too well the implications of an improper study of the Word. There were those in this country who used the Bible as a source for the teaching that African people were cursed with the descendants of Ham and that it was God's will for these descendants to be "hewers" (cutters) of wood and drawers of water. Others said that the dark-skinned people descended from the race of Cain and were not human but beasts. Since salvation came to the Adamic race, Cain's descendants had been left without hope.

Amid these skewed readings and interpretations, each of us must know the Word for ourselves. The Word declares that God has made of one blood all who dwell on the face of the earth (Acts 17:26) and that God is no respecter of persons (Acts 10:34). There are those who have taught and still teach that some are predestined for salvation while others are predestined for damnation. But we read that Jesus cried, "Come unto me, all ye that labor and are heavy laden, and I will give you rest" (Matthew 11:28) and that those who come to him, he "will in no wise cast out" (John 6:37).

Studying the Word of God enables us to get insight into the meaning and purpose of life not from the culture but from the Creator. As one scholar of the church put it, "from God alone can God be known." The straight gate and the narrow way that lead to life are found through the illumination of the Word (Matthew 7:13-14).

A second commitment is to religiously educate our children. Children are to be taught their value and worth in the sight of God. They do not come into the world with an intrinsic sense of worth; they do not enter the world with any innate desire to do things that are right. A child has the capacity for behaving like a wolf or a dog. Thus children must be taught what it means to bear the image of God. Dignity in character, purpose for life, esteem of self, and respect for others do not come about automatically. Through religious instruction, we prepare our children to seek the Lord, who brings salvation.

The Covenant calls for us to take an active role in educating our children. We dare not assume that they will turn out all right without religious guidance. Short of providing such guidance, we have threatened their souls, their lives, their well-being. And so we covenant to provide our children with instruction that is basic to self-understanding, that puts them in a proper relationship with God, fellow human beings, and the world, and that invites them to call upon God for salvation.

ד.ד

For Reflection and Discussion

- What are the benefits of every believer having access to the Scriptures? How can we protect against incorrect interpretations or applications of the Word?
- How do you study the Word? What resources do you use? What habits have you formed?

14

Seek the Salvation of Others

Lesson: John 20

Jesus saith unto her [Mary Magdalene], ... go to my brethren, and say unto them, I ascend unto my Father, and your Father; and to my God, and your God.... But these [signs] are written, that ye might believe that Jesus is the Christ, the Son of God; and that believing ye might have life through his name. (JOHN 20:17,31)

"We also engage ... to seek the salvation of our kindred and acquaintance."

Following his resurrection, Jesus made himself known first to those who were closest to him. Mary was the first to reach the tomb. Jesus instructed her to go tell the disciples the good news. This section of the Covenant affords us the opportunity to follow in Mary's footsteps, to bear witness to others (in this case, those among whom we have influence) that the Lord is risen and we have seen him. He has appeared, breaking the shackles of fear and bondage. He has appeared to end the long night of weeping. Though it endured for a night, the weeping gave way to the joy of the morning (Psalm 30:5).

At the very heart of faith is a mystery from which we dare not retreat. As the epistle writer put it, "God was manifest in the flesh, justified in the Spirit, seen of angels, preached unto the Gentiles, believed on in the world, received up into glory" (1 Timothy 3:16). Obstetrics notwithstanding, the secret has not been revealed concerning how the Spirit prepared a body in the virgin womb of Mary. Despite forays into anthropology, we do not have details concerning how the Spirit empowered Jesus to heal the sick and raise the dead. Even when pressed, mortuary science cannot explain how Jesus' own corpse, drained of blood and water and entombed three days, received new life. As mystery, these mighty works can never fully be explained. They must be confessed.

What we have in Scripture are witnesses who declare this truth, and the fact is they were transformed by their encounter with the risen Lord. The transformation continued within those who believed the report. Telling and believing the report, in the final analysis, is what advances the kingdom of our Lord. Power is released in telling the story to transform lives and to set men and women free.

Salvation comes through believing in the heart that God raised Jesus from the dead and through confessing that Jesus is Lord (Romans 10: 8-10). Through faith we are raised from the deadness of sin, united with Christ in baptism and res-urrection to walk in newness of life. This evangel (good news) requires an evangelist who is a witness to the saving grace and willing to make a report on what has been seen, heard, and felt.

As with other instruction in the Covenant, seeking the sal-vation of our kindred and acquaintance is much more easily said than done. The crusade evangelist can testify to God's power, invite people to accept Christ as Savior, and then move on to the next town. But for those representing Christ in their families, communities, or places of work, their lives are always on display. To be effective in seeking the salvation of those who know us, we must have something to show for our faith. We are always on the spot. After all, we can talk all we please about how good a commodity is, but at some point we have to either put up or shut up.

So how do we seek the salvation of kindred and acquaintances? Do we preach to them in each waking moment, telling them they need to be saved? Most likely, such a strategy will only ensure that they stay out of our path or perhaps even tell us off! Even in the midst of our imperfections we can strive to be loyal friends and loving, caring companions. As opportunities present themselves, we tell them about Jesus. We credit God for the wondrous works wrought among us. We demonstrate our faith and reliance on God in the midst of our trials, stresses, and difficulties. We go to God in prayer and give the evidence of the wondrous grace in healing our sickness, directing decisions, and granting us courage and strength in times of trouble.

In addition, we can exercise the power of intercessory prayer. We have been granted authority to pray for others, believing that God will save and heal another as a result of our faith and persistence (Mark 2:5). Chances are that many in your covenant community came to Christ because someone interceded on their behalf and would not give up until they came to saving faith.

Perhaps the most difficult part of seeking the salvation of friends and acquaintances is waiting for the Lord to do the work. Waiting, that is, without worrying, without giving up.

As we wait we would do well to remember those who waited for us. Seek the salvation of kinfolk and acquaintance. Be sensitive, patient, open to the Lord's leading. Be persistent, and trust God to do the rest.

⊁⊰

For Reflection and Discussion

- How is it possible to be a witness to those who know us best, despite our imperfections?
- What are the most common mistakes we make in witnessing to kinfolk? What kinds of issues do you struggle with in this area?
- How were you won to Christ? Was it because of someone you were close to? Did someone intercede on your behalf?

⋛ 15 ⋚

Walk Circumspectly

Lesson: Ephesians 5:8-20

But now are ye light in the Lord: walk as children of light; ...
Walk circumspectly, not as fools, but as wise, redeeming the
time, because the days are evil. (EPHESIANS 5:8,15-16)

"We also engage ... to walk circumspectly in the world."

The instruction to walk circumspectly summarizes the text in
Ephesians that deals with factors which determine how we
will be seen in the world. To walk circumspectly is to walk
carefully, cautiously, looking around at all sides. Paul makes
it clear that such a way of walking is not optional for those
who would please the Lord. In fact, those who refuse to live
up to standard are informed beyond a shadow of a doubt that
disobedience to the way of righteousness amounts to forfei-
ture of any inheritance in the kingdom of God.

Walking circumspectly means fundamentally that we are to
have no fellowship with the unfruitful works of darkness and
that we are to give no place to the devil (Ephesians 5:11;

4:27). To walk circumspectly is to walk straight. It is to live in such a way that we don't have to spend all our time defending our behavior. God does not need a church on the defensive, justifying itself against the charges of the world. Instead, the conversation concerning the church needs to be a good report that commends it for its walk with God.

First, walking circumspectly requires us to wake up: "Awake thou that sleepest, and arise from the dead, and Christ shall give thee light" (Ephesians 5:14). We must be awake to see danger and to mount a defense. Those who sleep may miss the opportunity that comes only once in a lifetime. In this crucial point in history, it is especially important for the church to be awake. It is only in a spiritually awakened, spiritually sensitive state that we are able to see and respond to the needs among us and around us, needs within the fold and outside.

The states of being asleep and being awake are contrasting ones. In both cases the body has the same potential, but in the sleeping state the body's power is not available. Critical information is bypassed; unrepeatable opportunities are lost. Thus, shaking to awaken opens the door to effective ministry. The Lord is calling the church to a spiritually awakened state where we see and respond to the needs among us. And God's first move to get us ready for those we must seek is to awaken us for the circumspect walk.

Second, walking circumspectly requires that we check up—on ourselves. Checking up is about accountability, about how we are using the time allotted to us. And we check up most effectively by redeeming time. Because the days are evil, the luxury of postponement is not permitted to the covenant community of faith. God gives us this moment, in which we can act wisely by the grace that has been given or in which we can waste time backtracking, repairing, and mending. We redeem time by turning from the temptation from which there is no remedy and pursuing the excellent way of reconciliation, love, and obedience.

Third, walking circumspectly requires us to fill up—but to fill up on the right source of intoxication. This involves coming under the control of the right power. We must acknowledge that we have a foe we cannot face in our power, a battle we cannot win by our strategy, and a score we cannot settle on our terms. Left to ourselves we will fail. We will be sleeping when we should be awake; we will miss moments of great opportunity. The victories we seek come not by our might. Thus the epistle writer enjoins us to fill up, to be filled with the Spirit, who empowers us takes control, and imparts vitality for the life of obedience and service. Being filled with the Spirit means that God can have his way with us at any time and in any circumstance. That being the case, it is impossible not to walk circumspectly.

There is nothing we can do about the past. But the future is open. If our walk is crooked, now is the time to get it straight. If it is straight, this is no time to change. Walking circumspectly is the only way to walk with the Lord.

➤.➤

For Reflection and Discussion

- The literal meaning of "circumspect" has to do with looking all around or watching all sides. How does this apply to the admonition of the Covenant?
- How might walking circumspectly relate to seeking the salvation of our kindred and acquaintance?
- Where in your life are you challenged to walk circumspectly?

⊒ 16 ⊑

Be Just and Faithful in Service

Lessons: 1 Thessalonians 4; Ephesians 4;
2 Thessalonians 3

As a prisoner for the Lord, then, I urge you to live a life
worthy of the calling you have received.... Make every
effort to keep the unity of the Spirit through the bond of
peace. (EPHESIANS 4:1,3, NIV)

"We engage ... to be kind and just to those in our employ, and
faithful in the service we promise others."

This phrase in the Covenant calls attention to the fact that salvation is not something we can put down when we get to our
job and pick back up when we come home. Indeed, at work—
under stress, in those moments when we are tested sorely—is
where we prove the quality of what we are given by Christ.

The focus of the Covenant is on kindness, justice, and
honest work ("faithful in the service we promise others").
Our behavior relative to these requirements will either
enhance the shining of the light given us or dim it under the

bushel. We who are in the fold may place a premium on what salvation does for us in the church—in worship. But this means little to those who need to be persuaded that ours is the good way. They are more interested in knowing what salvation has to offer in everyday trials of life than in how it affects us in church.

The Covenant calls us to a wholesome Christian attitude toward work, which for many is a challenging admonition. For some, work is an arena in which creativity flourishes and unfettered spirits soar. But for many others, work, quite frankly, is a drag. It is what we do because we have to in order to survive.

Work can be especially difficult when we are treated unfairly. Indeed, there are some aspects in the whole enterprise of work that seem unfair. Sometimes it seems that those who produce nothing live better than those who work hard. Business tycoons, entertainers, sports figures, investors, drug lords, pushers, pimps, and hustlers glitter in the financial limelight of our time. It is easy to become cynical and embittered, determined to get over the best way we can or to scheme in order to find our personal advantage. This provides incentive for gambling. We must recognize, however, that this kind of attitude injures our character, deforms our moral fiber, and makes us insensitive to the influences of the Spirit.

We are called to stand against the tide of the world, whether we are among the few who employ others or whether we, like most, are employed by another. To be kind and just to those in our employ presents a marvelous opportunity to witness to the character of Christ. So often in the working world employees are treated as mere commodities, line items on a balance sheet. The boss has little or no concern for employees as persons but cares only about what those employees can produce for the company. Often work environments are controlled by political considerations instead of by what is fair or just.

As believers we are called to a different standard. It is our responsibility to care about employees, their families, and their well-being not because they can help us make money but because they are created in the image of God. We are to model kindness and fairness at every turn. Ironically, most employers will discover that if they treat their employees with genuine concern, production will increase naturally. For believers, however, the injunction to treat others with kindness and justice is not a means to an end but an end in itself.

Then the Covenant enjoins us to be faithful in the service we promise others. To put it another way, we have the responsibility to put in an honest day's work. When we take a job, we promise to work for our wages. This itself is a contract, a covenant of sorts. The point is not to find the lowest rate of work and the least we can do. Rather, we are to do what is expected and to work at a reasonable pace. Christians should not need someone standing over them all day, looking over their shoulder, peeping every moment to see whether they are wasting time.

In addressing the Thessalonians, Paul not once but twice pleads in essence, "Darlings, don't be lazy and trifling ... you are messing yourselves up if you don't work." Apparently there were some in the church who were too spiritual to work. They were expecting the Lord to come back any time, so why work? But they had to eat, so they began bumming off others. What's more, in their idleness they were getting into trouble, behaving in disorderly ways. They gradually turned into busybodies. Paul knew that you can't form character in people who won't work (1 Thessalonians 4:11-12; 2 Thessalonians 3:10-13).

No light shines from our life if we work with resentment and disgust. True, the work may not be what we desire, but until we can do better we need to hold on to what we have. There is no need to be ashamed of our work if it is honest. Indeed, work is one of the ways by which the human creature is mediated to the world. Contrary to what we have sometimes been taught, work is not a curse from God. The curse comes in the resistance of the earth to the efforts at tilling (Genesis 3:17-19).

But as we advocate kindness and justice by employers, we must also teach employees within the fold that they are entitled to kind and just treatment. What we see within many sectors of the culture is a carryover of the false notion that God created some to be masters and some to be slaves, some to rule and some to serve. The notion continues, saying that God created a race of people in fixed stations and that removing one's self from such a station is a violation of the eternal decree. These arguments were used as built-in protection for the systems of serfdom and slavery. They were trotted out to deter the advance of organized labor. They are being used once again to justify the free-wage slavery governing our present economy. We must be clear that there are no black jobs and white jobs. God didn't predestine anybody to poverty.

The time is past for the slavery-time notion that because people are Christians they are supposed to let themselves be kicked around like dogs. Being saved doesn't make you somebody's doormat. Many people will be turned from the faith if they are shown that being a Christian means you must let someone walk all over you because you belong to Christ. You don't have to put your salvation on hold to stand up for your dignity; that's when you need spiritual boldness most!

This is not to say that we should go to work on Monday with a rude and surly disposition, ready to confront the supervisor at the first provocation. But neither should we assume that because we are in Christ we must grovel and crawl before so-called superiors who feed their egos at our expense. With all the dignity and grace God gives, employees need to stand up for their rights. Demand respect by the way you carry yourself. Do your work so that nobody can find fault with you. Let your godly manner be your vindication. Refuse to sign erroneous evaluations. Pursue the redress that is available when mistreated. As occasion affords, look to upgrade. Don't assume another has an entitlement that does not also belong to you.

You will be surprised at what God can do through your life if you do your best to follow the injunction in the Covenant to treat others with kindness and justice, to expect the same from others, and to work hard for the wages you earn—and for the glory your service brings to God.

➤∎◄

For Reflection and Discussion

- What are some specific things employers can do to show they truly care about their workers?
- In what ways is the value of an honest day's work slipping away from our culture?
- No work environment will be perfect. But where do you draw the line between being a patient, faithful employee and standing up for your rights?

⊒ 17 ⊑

Commend Our Holy Faith

Lessons: Acts 20:28-38; 2 Corinthians 5

Now then we are ambassadors for Christ. (2 CORINTHIANS 5:20)

➤∎◂

"... endeavoring in the purity of heart and good will ... to exemplify and commend our holy faith."

How do we make somebody want to be a Christian? How do we live so others want to be like us? This is the question we ponder in this phrase of the Covenant. This is not a complicated theological or doctrinal issue. Rather, we have come to the nitty gritty, as we sometimes call it. The challenge is to put our holy faith on display in a manner that commends it to others.

To succeed at commending our faith requires that we be able to deliver what we promise, to produce what we have advertised. There is no room for discrepancy between what we claim and the way we live. If we have passed from death to life, we must love our brothers and sisters. If we truly love the Lord, we will keep his commandments. After all, the Lord linked the believability of the gospel to our unity. His closing prayer for the disciples was for the Father to make them one so that the world might believe he had indeed been sent (John 17:6-26, especially v. 22).

In the text from Acts we see the apostle Paul making his rounds among churches that had been established by his gospel labors. His purpose was to reach Jerusalem by Pentecost. From Miletus Paul sent for the elders of the church at Ephesus so he could bid them farewell for the last time. He reviewed his work among them—how he had preached the gospel of the kingdom, how he had walked in purity among them, and how he had not failed to declare the full counsel of God. Having exemplified his faith, Paul commended it to them, knowing that this holy faith would sustain them though wolves came into their midsts. He offered his life as a witness that God could build them up in any circumstance and give them an inheritance among those who are sanctified (Acts 26:18).

We promise so much in the name of the Lord: salvation, fullness of joy, care for the lost, comfort for those who mourn, food for the hungry, clothes for the naked. But here we must ask how much we deliver. What do we offer, for example, to someone attempting to decide whether to be a Christian or a Muslim? What do we say to someone on our side of town contemplating whether to unite with our church or to travel past us on their way to another church? What do we say to our children once they turn eighteen or twenty-one and we can no longer compel them to go to church? And how do we persuade those who are walking in the darkness of sin that the church is a "happening place"?

This challenge is greater than ever in a civilization that does its business without honoring God. The cult of self-sufficiency is still thriving for some. People not hit by the downturn of the economy are doing quite well, and they believe others are just trifling. Folks fare well so long as the doctor can diagnose their ailment and prescribe a sufficient cure. How do you commend faith to them?

The Covenant calls us to purity of heart and good will as prerequisites in exemplifying the holy faith. We are told in Matthew 5:8 that only with purity of heart shall we see God. To be pure in heart means that our motives, our intentions must be genuine, unfeigned. We cannot be guilty of pretense or hypocrisy. We must do what we do aboveboard, being honest and forthright in our dealings with others. We are reminded of the words of the Lord when he declared that unless we become like children we cannot enter the kingdom of heaven (Matthew 18:3). The child does not know how to pretend. When the heart is pure, righteousness is no longer a matter of formality; it is the product of faith. It flows from the abundance of the heart (Matthew 12:34).

A clean heart and a right spirit are the fundamental conditions for offering goodwill to others. Things will not work right until hearts are cleansed. But a pure heart is the result of a spiritual pilgrimage. We cannot rest on previous experience, no matter how intense or memorable. Purity of heart requires fresh applications of grace, constant exposure to the cleansing stream, for it is too easy for motives to become corrupted.

We may be victims of lies, scandals, or other forms of mistreatment. But it is our duty to see to it that every bad report is a false report. Remember, we are not exemplifying and commending ourselves but representing the one who claims power sufficient to transform a life, a community, and ultimately all of creation.

The challenge related to commending our faith is that we do not always know how. For example, sometimes we feel like we just want to pour salvation into somebody. We know what they need, but they don't. People come with a steady barrage of questions and problems. We love them, so we listen and do all we can to help. All the while you know what the problem is. A good dose of salvation will straighten them out. But knowing how to get this message across is not always easy or obvious. Should we be direct, to the point? Or ought we be content in testifying what the Lord has done for us? Are there times when we should say or do nothing?

There are no easy answers. There is no clear right and wrong. The important thing, however, is the desire to commend our faith to others and to do so with a pure heart. We must not back away from troubles or cower at the challenge of the Enemy. In prayer, we pull down the Enemy's strongholds and rebuke contrary spirits.

Most of all, we must remember that the level of spiritual power we need to adequately commend the faith cannot come from ourselves. Nor will it come to us automatically just because we have confessed Jesus as Lord and been baptized and joined the church. We must grow in grace, seeking purity of heart, following the Lord in traveling the path of the just that shines more and more unto that perfect day (2 Peter 3:18; see also 1 Kings 19:18).

ᴙ.ᴙ

For Reflection and Discussion

- Whom have you known in the past or present who represents purity of heart? What are the characteristics of this person?
- How is it possible to commend the faith even though we are flawed human beings?

≡ 18 ≡

Watch Over and Stir Up Each Other

Lessons: 2 Timothy 4; 2 Timothy 1

For this reason I remind you to fan into flame the gift of God, which is in you through the laying on of my hands. (2 TIMOTHY 1:6, NIV)

➤.◄

"We further engage to watch over, to pray for, to exhort and stir up each other unto every good word and work."

According to the Covenant, various responsibilities we have to one another are not optional. To be united in the Spirit is not something for us to consider. Rather, it is commanded of us. A church will never be as strong and vibrant in the service of God as it ought to be until it shares in this ministry of watching over and stirring up one another.

Let's be clear, however, that being involved in the lives of others does not mean we should be nosy, gossiping, poking into other folks' business. No, we are called to be involved as caring people under God. Thus we must constantly assess our motives, for example, for wanting to know more about a particular situation.

We are mandated under God not to idly allow a soul to perish—especially one who has confessed Christ. In part, this means reminding others of who we are in Christ and admonishing them to live by this power. Watching over entails coming to the aid of the one in need of assistance, whether it is spiritual or temporal. This work takes seriously what it means to be baptized into Christ. For it is through baptism that we are mystically joined to Christ by the power of the Holy Spirit. Again, by this same mystery we are joined to one another. We are not our own.

In a very real sense, those who are joined to Christ give up autonomy for communion with others who believe. Wherever we go and in everything we do, we represent Christ and the body to which we have been joined (Ephesians 5:29-32). This idea strikes at the heart of the cherished American value of privacy. We are conditioned in this culture to mind our own business. The Covenant instructs us that our business sometimes means caring about other people's business too. From the beginning of humanity, God has called people to watch after others. It is clear that the answer to Cain's question, "Am I my brother's keeper?" was yes (Genesis 4:9-10).

The root of this watch-care is the all-seeing eye of God—and the emphasis of that divine observation is on care, or careful watching. Watchful caring entails noticing one another, paying attention to another's state of mind and needs. It entails looking for evidence of spiritual growth or slippage and responding accordingly. It is not a matter of prying into another's business but rather of spiritual sensitivity. Thus we are to miss the brother or sister who we do not see in worship, prayer, and Bible study. We are to be sensitive to the broken spirit, the troubled countenance, and the cry of distress. Not every sound we hear in the house is a sound of rejoicing. We need to know that some cries are laments.

This responsibility for careful watching is given to all who are bound by this Covenant. It is not just the work of the pastor, deacons, and associate ministers. It is not reserved for the church's elected officials. No, this is the way all within the body are to behave toward one another, even though some may have primary responsibility for this work. Let us not forget that church leaders, like everyone else, need people to look after them with watchful caring.

The preacher needs someone watching for him or her when standing before the congregation to declare the Word. Keep in mind that there are some messages the Enemy does not want to go forth. The pastor needs people who are watching, who can go to God in intercession without having to be told and without needing to know all the details.

When prayer is involved, watching with care is clearly distinguished from the nosy sort of watching. Taking the posture of the intercessor signifies pure motives. In this regard, we sometimes underestimate the power of prayer. "All we can do is pray," we say, suggesting a sigh of resignation. In fact, prayer is a powerful response to the challenge of watching after others. It is not just saying words, but rather it is entering the world, the life, the space of others and carrying them into the presence of God (James 5:14-16).

Intercessory prayer is not merely some stopgap measure we invoke when we have tried everything and all else has failed. It should not be considered a last resort but a first resort. It strengthens and supports all other efforts. Whether praying for the sick or the weak in faith, praying at the beginning of worship or before a meeting, praying at the start of the day or before a meal, prayer is serious work, as serious as anything we can attempt to do.

Watching with care sometimes requires the prophetic gift of exhortation. For some this concept of exhortation brings to mind negative images, such as telling someone off or giving someone a piece of our mind. But properly understood, exhortation encourages, uplifts, and mediates confidence and strength (1 Corinthians 14:3). People are strengthened to hold on to God when they receive exhortation from someone who believes in them. We all have low moments, times when we feel like quitting. A positive word of exhortation can make all the difference. It has the power to turn us back toward God and to encourage us in our efforts to travel on the path of righteousness.

A word that exhorts often reminds us that we are not alone. Others have gone before us, and they came forth in victory. This is the power of the Christian testimony: it proclaims that God has done it before and can be counted on to do it again.

As for the gift of stirring up, it is nothing short of amazing what one person can do to influence others when he or she has it. God has given us the power to stir up one another for good works, and to some the gift has been given in abundant measure. We need to seek the Lord to know our gift and to cultivate it. Most likely we all know someone who has the gift of stirring up. Perhaps she or he is not gifted to teach, dissect problems, or pinpoint the source of spiritual conflict. But that person is capable of stirring up others who can.

To be about this ministry requires belief in someone other than ourselves. We must remember the way over which we have come in the Lord. This prompts us to comfort others with the same comfort we have received (2 Corinthians 1:3-4). But it also reminds us that God wills the growth of another as much as God wills ours.

Paul understood well this ministry as he spoke to the young preacher Timothy, whom he had left in Ephesus. He spoke words to stir up the young man. He reminded him of the faith that was in his mother and his grandmother, being fully persuaded that the same faith was in him. He went further to recall the moment when he made the good confession of faith and when hands were laid on him, accompanied by prophetic utterance. On the strength of the remembrance, Paul admonished Timothy to stir up the gift that was within him (2 Timothy 1:6).

Perhaps God is calling you to this ministry of stirring up one another to good work. Sometimes we feel the Spirit stirring within us, but we quench it due to concern for how it will make us appear to another. It may well be that God wants to use our praise to stir up someone who wants to be free in the Lord. God may want to use our song to encourage another to sing.

Let the Spirit take control: you will find yourself getting stirred up when you wanted to be cool, speaking up when you preferred to be quiet. To watch over, pray for, exhort, and stir up others is everyone's responsibility. But to some, these capacities may also be a special gift.

⁊.⹁

For Reflection and Discussion

- What are some principles for distinguishing between watching over others and poking into other people's business?

- In your experience, have you found it the case that many think looking out for others is a job for just the pastor and deacons? How can this be changed?
- Is there anyone you are watching over, praying for in particular? Who has watched over you?
- How have you been encouraged by someone's positive words of exhortation?
- Do you know of someone who has the gift of stirring up? Can anyone potentially claim this gift? Have you considered whether it might be your gift?

⹅ **19** ⹅

Guard Each Other's Reputation

Lessons: Romans 15; Acts 2:1-11

We then that are strong ought to bear the infirmities of the weak, and not to please ourselves. Let every one of us please his neighbor for his good to edification. For even Christ pleased not himself; but, as it is written, The reproaches of them that reproached thee fell on me. (ROMANS 15:1-3)

"We further engage ... to guard each other's reputation, not necessarily exposing the infirmities of others."

This section of the Covenant moves us even deeper into the interior of our life together in Christ. It enables us to discover the intricate, delicate nature of the relationships that exist among us as members of the covenant community when our ways are pleasing to the Lord. We are enjoined in essence to be guardians of the reputation and infirmities of others.

In the Scripture text, the apostle is struggling with the church in Rome to keep the inner bonds of affection among them strong. From his seat in prison he could especially appreciate the great gift of fellowship afforded believers when they allowed the Spirit to flow. He knew what it was like to have fellow believers stab him in the back and become the cause of his persecution. He also knew the untold strength that comes when brothers and sisters bear up one another in Christ by the power of the Holy Spirit.

In essence, Paul advocates the principle of unselfishness for the good of all. We care for each other in part by guarding one another's reputation. We are called to take a stand against sinful human nature, which leads to gossip and demeaning others, sometimes demolishing others to enhance our egos. The Covenant calls us to a different standard. In fact, it ought to be a painful thing for us to see the name of a brother or a sister in Christ dragged through the mud.

Protecting others goes beyond declining to engage in behavior that tears another down. It also means working to build others up in their character and in their reputation or the way they are perceived. We must ask ourselves, "When I have the opportunity to say something about a brother or sister, what do I say?" The Covenant calls us to say things that promote peace, harmony, good will, and mutual affection.

The reputation—a good name or good report—is to be highly treasured by the believer. According to Proverbs 22:1, a good name is to be preferred above riches. A good reputation can open doors that money cannot unlock; it can commend us when other assets are of no avail.

By contrast, our opportunities to succeed in life and ministry are limited if a bad reputation precedes us. There are those who will not give us the time of day if the wrong report arrives before we do. Sometimes we may even decline the opportunity to get to know a brother or a sister because of something we heard about that person. This is the case even though there are people in all our lives to whom we have said, "You are not at all like they said you were like."

The injunction to guard reputations has personal and corporate dimensions. That is, we are to guard the reputation of our church and the church of God as a whole, knowing that men and women make their decisions concerning the faith based on what they see and believe about the church. They may not get to see for themselves if what they hear is too discouraging.

Guarding the reputation of others and of the church will sometimes mean stopping potentially damaging reports dead in their tracks. We owe it to one another to take a stand. This may mean we have to take a risk on occasion by standing up for a brother or a sister we may not know that well. We need to take such risks, even though we might sometimes prove to be wrong. Until we know the full story, we need to give each other the benefit of the doubt.

This is not to say we should lie or attempt to cover up improper behavior. But we need to guard against the trick of the Enemy to undermine the church through the creation and spreading of false tales. The Enemy seeks to sow discord and distrust among those sworn to put his mess out of business (Proverbs 6:19). A little dissention here, a little rumor there, a little rift over yonder, and all of our attention is diverted. While we are preoccupied, the Enemy can run wild: souls languish in bondage, and suffering ones are left to go through it alone.

Notice that the Covenant candidly acknowledges that we have weaknesses, infirmities. Thus bearing up one another requires relationships of trust in which we touch others in our tenderness without needlessly exposing these infirmities. As much as some of us hate to admit it, we are delicate. We cover over our tender spots with tough talk and bad acting. But we are just fooling ourselves. Indeed, a lot of the trouble into which we enter results from refusing to acknowledge our weaknesses and to find help. In so doing we shield ourselves from the true source of our help. In the meantime, we treat our weaknesses defensively—covering them, making excuses, justifying them because others have the same or worse ones. Then we become adversaries with those who know us intimately; we fall prey to the threats predicated on their knowledge.

We need relationships where we are honest enough with one another to give helpful feedback. Part of guarding one another involves cultivating relationships that are strong enough to bear the truth, even when it is unpleasant. But the point is that our infirmities, flaws in judgment, and imperfections in temperament need not have an impact on our reputation. They can be admitted and dealt with as infirmities by those who care for us and who will not expose them to those who would destroy us.

In caring for one another in the midst of infirmities, we need to see Jesus on the cross. He takes our infirmities, our weaknesses, and our shortcomings. He exposes them not to the world but to the Father. He exposes them not as ours but as his. He pays the price, he dies the death, and he wins the victory. Surely he has borne our grief and carried our sorrows. He was wounded for our transgressions; he was bruised for our iniquities (Isaiah 53:4; 63:1-3). This is why it is unnecessary to expose the infirmities, the shortcomings of those who are attempting to follow Jesus.

May we seek the power of the Spirit, who gives us the capacity and the disposition to bear one another up, to guard each other's reputation, even in the presence of infirmities.

➤∎◄

For Reflection and Discussion

- Describe a situation when you had an impression of someone based on his or her reputation only to find out that your first impression was wrong.
- What are some specific ways in which believers can guard each other's reputations?
- How can a bad reputation for a church influence its ability to minister effectively?
- How can the church deal with people's flaws without soiling the reputation of the covenant community or of the individuals themselves?
- What are some principles for distinguishing between situations where a person's shortcomings should be kept private and when misbehavior needs to be brought out into the open?

20

Participate in Each Other's Joy

Lesson: Philippians 2:1-18

Then make my joy complete by being like-minded, having the same love, being one in spirit and purpose. Do nothing out of selfish ambition or vain conceit, but in humility consider others better than yourselves. (PHILIPPIANS 2:2-3, NIV)

⚊⚊

"We further engage ... to participate in each other's joy, and with tender sympathy bear one another's burdens and sorrows."

One of the saddest traps in life is the hedonistic tendency that sends us in the wrong direction to search for joy. The fullest joy of life is not found in selfish ventures. We achieve it instead by building up others, helping others to find fulfillment.

We are called by the Covenant to participate in the experiences of others, whether they are joyful or sorrowful.

Empathizing with others and living for others takes us into one of the deepest dimensions of love—to a point where our lives intersect, join, flow through one another in communion. Within the body of Christ we know this movement as the "koinonia of the Spirit." There is really no other way to be built up in the faith (2 Corinthians 13:14).

On the surface, it may seem easier to participate in the joys of others than to participate in their sorrows. But for some the opposite is true. Yes, there are those who can weep with others but who cannot rejoice. In some cases persons are so used to being down they do not know how to act when they are afforded the privilege of getting up. Others may have a jealous spirit; they cannot stand to see another doing well. But weeping with those who weep is not so difficult; often it is almost natural.

The instruction to participate in the joys of one another is a call to a plane of fellowship that rules out jealousy, covetousness, and ill will. When these vices are present within us, we are tempted to be joyful when the ones we despise suffer hardship, disappointment, or tragedy. Perhaps somewhere in the back of our minds we feel they deserve what is coming to them for the way they treated us. It is all but impossible to not be joyful at the misery of people who have been the source of so much mistreatment, grief, and harshness.

But love calls us to rise above our resentment, jealousy, covetousness, and anger with the way we have been treated. Participating in the joy of the other—for some, a challenging discipline—builds up the common life; it increases our love and, if we allow it, fulfills our joy.

As we participate in the joys of others we have the opportunity to be encouraged, strengthened. I will always recall the experience I had when finishing my doctoral studies. My office was directly across the hall from where the final exams were given. I would sit there and watch candidates enter and leave. Before I finished, it gave me joy to see that someone else had completed his or her course. What gave me great joy was reassurance that the task was doable.

When God makes a way for another, that should increase our joy. When persons go through sickness, falling to the door of death only to have the Lord bring them back, that is to be joy for us all. When we have prayed for God to move in a hard matter and after waiting patiently we see the signs of the Almighty working, we should rejoice. If we shut off the flow of joy, we deprive ourselves.

Let us not be like the Pharisees, who scorned Jesus for the time he took with publicans, harlots, and sinners. With their crusty rituals, cold religion, and vindictive spirits, they shut out the flow of joy in their lives. They were content to bind phylacteries about their heads, to wear long, flowing robes in public, and to put down others for a favorable comparison. But there was nothing in their worship to commend it to others. It was devoid of joy. It caused them pain when sinners came into the presence of Jesus, found forgiveness, and experienced an overflow of joy.

We will be a better people when we intensify our search for ways to participate in the joy of others. Indeed, participating with others is also to be the aim of our sympathy, of bearing one another's burdens and sorrows. We were never promised a life free of pain and disappointment.

When times of pain come, we are called to be there for one another to offer spiritual and material support. No one in the church should have to bear pain, grief, and disappointment alone. It is the responsibility of the church to be present with those in pain, to look after their practical needs, or perhaps to listen or to allow another to weep in our presence. Those who can relate to the pinch, the pain, the utter hurt especially need to be there to minister in the midst of the agony of those who are going through.

But even in ministering to those in the midst of sickness, pain, or grief, the goal is to return to joy. We don't help others by allowing them to wallow in their sorrow. Our task is to lead brothers and sisters through their sorrows to the joy offered by the Lord for our strength.

There is a door in every circumstance. It makes no difference how deep the sorrow might be or how long it has lasted. The door that opens is not always one that can be seen: tears can cloud our vision. Assessment of the practical factors or judgment by feeble sense can put a fog in the atmosphere, leaving us overcast by a pall of doubt. But we serve a Savior who has passed through the bitter pangs of death and who is able to come to us from the other side of sorrow. The door is known to the Master, who is the resurrection and the life, and who holds the keys to death, hell, and the grave (John 11:25; Revelation 1:8). From the other side of the sorrow, he comes to us as the huddle of doubting disciples and breathes upon us the Spirit of joy (John 20:26). Thus we proclaim that joy can come from sorrow.

Whatever the source of the joy, we are enjoined to participate in it. The joy of one is bound up with the joy of another—indeed, of *all* others in the church. So when the joy comes, participate in it! Don't block it. Move with God's Spirit. Receive all the joy God offers, no matter what the direction of the flow.

For Reflection and Discussion

- Do you know people for whom it is easier to weep than to rejoice? Why is this the case? How can someone overcome this tendency and learn to be joyful?
- In what ways have you participated in the joys of others? How have others participated in your joys?
- How have you seen God use pain and sorrow to bring people closer together and even to bring joy?

21

Cultivate Christian Courtesy

Lesson: Matthew 7:1-12

If ye then, being evil, know how to give good gifts unto your children, how much more shall your Father which is in heaven give good things to them that ask him? Therefore all things whatsoever ye would that men should do to you, do ye even so to them: for this is the law and the prophets. (MATTHEW 7:11-12)

"We further engage ... to cultivate Christian courtesy."

We all have some concept of common courtesy. Many people equate courtesy with good manners: saying please and thank you, respecting elders, treating others with respect. Without some notion of common courtesy, a community is in danger of collapsing.

In times past there was a consensus of sorts concerning what constituted common courtesy in our culture. Within the home, there was a threshold of respect given to adults that spilled over into the community. There was a way in which adults were to be addressed, and failure to do so yielded sure and swift consequences. Such consequences were meted out not just by parents but by neighbors and relatives as well.

It used to be taken for granted that children would refer to adults as Mr. or Mrs., rather than by their first name. Men opened the door for women without their having to ask. And everybody respected and assisted the elderly. There was a certain degree of honor associated with the offices or positions people held, whether they were preachers, teachers, deacons, or doctors. To be sure, we ought not glamorize some previous golden era, for surely there have always been liars, rowdy souls, and foul mouths. But our notion of common courtesy puts some space off limits with respect to certain behaviors.

As much as some might value common courtesy, however, the Covenant calls us to the higher standard of Christian courtesy. Perhaps the best way to understand the difference between the two is to focus on the distinction between a set of rules and a governing attitude. Common courtesy focuses on a prescribed set of rules to govern behavior. Christian courtesy is rooted in an attitude.

Jesus taught us how we should behave, especially in the Sermon on the Mount. Jesus set the instruction of this sermon against the background of Torah—the law of Moses. The law of Moses was given to establish order among persons who had been slaves and, before that, nomads wandering in the desert. In their world, those who were powerful and wealthy moved forcefully and swiftly to dominate the weaker ones among them.

To restrain behavior, the law of Moses required an eye for an eye, a tooth for a tooth, a limb for a limb, a life for a life. Those who were bold and brazen enough to commit acts that violated others were bound to suffer the same violence. This was law based on a principle of retributive justice: the threat of retribution was calculated to make persons pause and think before committing acts. Some people still promote this principle as the way to control crime and violence. Indeed, one of the biggest industries in many locales is that of building and operating prisons. (The tragic fact is that no sooner has one prison been filled than another is needed.)

Jesus' standard, in contrast, is based on the personal worth and value of those who are created and loved by the heavenly Father. The pinnacle of his instruction on how we should treat others consists of the Golden Rule: "Do to others what you would have them do to you" (Matthew 7:12, NIV). Indeed, this is the standard for Christian courtesy.

Christian courtesy begins with the unequaled love God has for all human beings. Jesus speaks of a father who will not give his son a stone when he asks for bread or a serpent when he asks for fish. But even an earthly father's love pales in comparison with the love of God. Human goodness cannot begin to approach the love God has for us. This is the affirmation that is to establish our value. We are to know it, accept it, feel it, be shaped by it. This sense of our value is to ricochet in our mind and permeate our conduct. And then it is to go forth by the power of the Spirit as Christian courtesy toward those possessing the same value in the sight of God.

Jesus was calling the world to a different, higher standard, reflected by the many times he said, "You have heard it said of old, but I say unto you...." What they had heard of old had to be infused with a greater degree of love and compassion. The righteousness called for by the Lord had to exceed that of the scribes and Pharisees (Matthew 5:20).

Christian courtesy is treating others as those who are as precious as we are in the sight of God. It translates into simple acts, not to be taken for granted: speaking kindly to another, paying attention to the needs of others. It means extending not the limp hand but the warm one; not the shifting eyes but the full, loving gaze; not avoidance but a holy embrace.

Jesus calls us to a courtesy that goes beyond common courtesy. He calls us to kingdom courtesy, which is anything but common. In fact, it is radical. He looked at people who were at the bottom rung of the social order and declared how precious they were in the sight of the heavenly Father. By no means wealthy, not holding the status of soldiers, having no claim to Roman citizenship, and not even having the status of slaves of the wealthy, they were the urban poor. With no land and no advocates, they were the prey of the Romans and the Jewish aristocracy. No doubt when Jesus said they were precious, they looked around wondering if he was speaking to them.

The Master told them that the Father cared for them more than the lilies of the field. He told them a sparrow cannot fall without God noticing it, and they were far more precious than that. Jesus said the heavenly Father was infinitely more loving toward them than the kindest father they knew (Matthew 6:25-34). Then he said to take this courtesy you have received and extend it to others.

Common courtesy is not a high enough standard. We are called to Christian courtesy, which radiates from those in whom the light of Christ shines. After all, we are people who know what it is to be loved and cherished by the heavenly Father and who learn from that love how to behave toward others.

For Reflection and Discussion

- What are some examples of common courtesy? How do they differ from the Christian courtesy the Covenant calls us to exhibit?
- In what understandings, theological truths, and teachings of Jesus is Christian courtesy based?

⇥ **22** ⇤

Be Slow to Give or Take Offense

Lesson: 2 Corinthians 5:12-21

And all things are of God, who hath reconciled us to himself by Jesus Christ, and hath given to us the ministry of reconciliation; to wit, that God was in Christ, reconciling the world unto himself, not imputing their trespasses unto them; and hath committed unto us the word of reconciliation. (2 CORINTHIANS 5:18-19)

"We further engage ... to be slow to give or take offense, but always ready for reconciliation."

Quiet as the secret may be kept, no aspect of our Christian life is more crucial for this worthy goal than being reconciled with God and with one another. Reconciliation is grounded in the work of Christ and is not something we achieve through our own efforts. But the task of reconciliation is our principle engagement as members of the covenant community. Spiritual power is forfeited if we fail to withstand the stresses of our common life together and allow fractures to rupture our unity. We feed our own weakness in moments when we take offense rather than praying for the offender and when we cling to our grudges instead of extending forgiveness. Power comes only when we go through the circumstances that were calculated to crush us.

Thus, to be reconciled and to remain reconciled, we engage, by the Spirit's aid, to be slow to give or take offense. As with other instruction in the Covenant, this task of avoiding offense—as giver or receiver—goes against the grain of our human tendencies. Early on, we learn that we "ain't supposed to take nothing from nobody." Soon little ones learn to talk junk—to pop off at the mouth or to make their case verbally and physically.

As adults, we are sometimes easily offended or easily offend others, including those close to us, based on such seemingly trivial matters as a tone of voice or nonverbal communication. We are prone to get upset if we are not recognized for something we have done or if we feel we are taken for granted, or not fully appreciated. There are a thousand and one ways in which we rub against and bombard one another in this intersection of physical and spiritual space that we know as a Christian community.

These seemingly mundane matters determine the temperature within our spiritual environment, for the Spirit cannot flow freely among hearts that are not turned toward one another in love and reconciliation (Malachi 4:5-6). Thus the admonition to be slow to give and take offense is a virtue with which to stamp our character.

We must go beyond avoiding certain behaviors or attitudes, for often we offend without even being aware of it. Thus we need to adopt a certain level of self-consciousness, accompanied by increased sensitivity to others. We must make an intentional effort to be aware of the impact we make through facial expressions, tone of voice, body language, or gestures. We need to know whether ours is the soft answer that turns away wrath or the grievous word that stirs up anger (Proverbs 15:1). We are admonished to be quick to hear, slow to speak, and slow to wrath, for our wrath does not produce God's righteousness (James 1:19-20).

Slowing the pace at which we give offense requires cultivation of the virtues of kindness and patience. This is fruit of the Spirit (Galatians 5:22-23), cultivated by the ambassador of reconciliation. It is grounded in Christ, who is our peace (Ephesians 2:14). We cultivate this virtue in practical ways, such as increasing reaction time. (Some might say we should count to ten.) This is to say that not everything is as it first seems to be. Yes, there is evil, and some of what comes our way is done with evil intent. But assuming evil intent need not and should not be our first response.

Instead of being anxious, ever ready to offend—or to conclude that another has offended us—we are instructed to be always ready, for reconciliation. This attitude is modeled by the apostle Paul, who chastised and encouraged the saints at Corinth through a somewhat painful letter. Grave problems of discipline existed among them, and some in the number challenged his authority to chastise. It seems that a prior correspondence prescribed discipline that caused considerable grief to Paul, to the congregation that dispensed it, and to the one who received it. The apostle wanted them to know that once the matter was handled there should be forgiveness and reconciliation.

In this epistle, the connection is made between mundane matters of personal conduct to the great theme of the reconciliation of the world in Christ. In cautioning the church, Paul observes how Satan delights in blinding our eyes from truth that is hidden in Christ. It is accomplished not by major theological controversy but by little distractions. Insignificant, temporal matters have eternal implications.

The bottom line is that we have been united with Christ, made new creatures, and reconciled to God. This truth is to govern the way we comprehend every ordeal of our lives, including the seemingly petty squabbles that keep us from being all we ought to be as individuals and as the body of Christ. As those who are reconciled to God, the love of Christ constrains us with power that exceeds every contrary force.

Theologically, in a real sense, what is at stake is the atonement. Because of Christ's atoning work, we are united with him and with one another. We are new creatures. Old things are passed away, and behold, all things become new. On the basis of this wonderful work we are given the ministry of reconciliation, and we are made ambassadors of reconciliation. When we achieve reconciliation, we testify to the power of atonement. The wall that would divide us has been torn from its foundation, broken down, ripped apart, and discarded as refuse.

We need to recognize this relationship between Jesus' work on the cross and the tiny acts that govern our behavior. This would give us a new disposition when we ponder our behavior, our reactions, our manners. More, this would become virtue within our character, the stamp upon us that identifies us to the world as the people of God.

In a sense, all of our worship—indeed, all of life in Christ—is but coming to and leaving the table of Communion. Here we bring as refuse all our sins; misdeeds, cares, and burdens are to be laid upon the one who died that we might be reconciled with God and with one another. He became sin for us that we might be the righteousness of God in him. Having received the grace to live as reconciled people, we go forth from the Table as ambassadors of this reconciliation.

➤◣◥

For Reflection and Discussion

- What principles can we apply to our lives to increase the capacity to be slow in taking offense?
- What are some reasons that we (or others) can offend (or be offended) without realizing it?
- How can seemingly trivial disputes affect the larger work of the church? Have you seen this happen?

23

Be Ready for Reconciliation

Lesson: Matthew 18:10-22

"If your brother sins against you, go and show him his fault, just between the two of you. If he listens to you, you have won your brother over. But if he will not listen, take one or two others along, so that 'every matter may be established by the testimony of two or three witnesses.' If he refuses to listen to them, tell it to the church; and if he refuses to listen even to the church, treat him as you would a pagan or a tax collector."
(MATTHEW 18:15-17, NIV)

"We further engage ... being mindful of the rules of the Saviour ..., to secure [reconciliation] without delay."

This phrase of the Covenant refers us to Matthew 18, where we find step-by-step, blow-by-blow instructions on how to handle those who get out of line in the church. It's a micromanual of sorts that covers conflict and church discipline. This manual prescribes three clear steps that presuppose a spirit of fellowship and harmony and that are given to maintain this spirit.

There are, however, other presuppositions contained within this text. One is that those who administer the discipline are right. Another is that brothers and sisters in Christ are to be able to face one another and talk things over as Christians. (Often, when this is done in a meek and prayerful spirit, nothing more is required.) A third presupposition is that fellowship in the church truly means something and, conversely, disfellowship constitutes a real penalty.

Conflict within the church is inevitable. As the Lord puts it, "It is impossible but that offenses will come" (Luke 17:1). The question is how we ought to address the conflict. The first principle for doing so is this: "If your brother sins against you, go and show him his fault, just between the two of you" (Matthew 18:15, NIV).

This is the simplest of remedies, and I daresay we underestimate how many problems this simple step would solve. It is staggering to think about how many people may be walking around in the church with hurt feelings—pouting, with mouths poked out, unwilling to serve. Often the person who offended them doesn't know it. We must face the reality that despite our unity in Christ we are not the same. We don't think alike, we have had different experiences, and we interpret things differently. I frequently laugh at myself when I make a goof. But I could laugh at someone else for making the same mistake and that person might be highly offended. This first principle for conflict resolution presumes that some problems are based on misunderstanding. Often a simple apology is all that is required.

Keep in mind, however, that apologizing and asking for pardon are not the same. An apology focuses on clarifying intent, whereas asking for pardon constitutes admitting that a wrong was done and asking for forgiveness. We ought not ask for pardon when we feel we have done nothing wrong, for such insincerity will not ultimately heal the relationship. Yet as Christians we must be willing to acknowledge when we have made a mistake. We ought not delude others by believing that we will make no mistakes because we are saved, sanctified, and filled with the Holy Ghost. In fact, one sign of the grace we have been given is being able to admit our faults and ask for forgiveness.

And so we should take seriously the biblical counsel to get with a brother or a sister and work things out, whether it's a matter of clarifying or asking forgiveness. Beyond the shortcomings in our behavior that are to be expected, however, there is another category of wrongdoing that is more brazen. In fact, there are some kinds of behavior for which we should have no tolerance. Some behavior has no place among the people of God, for at some point there has to be a difference between us and the world, between clean and unclean, holy and unholy. There is always room in the church for those who repent of past behavior regardless of its nature. But there is to be no comfort in the church for those who, for example, insist on being liars or thieves or fornicators or backbiters.

These can be sensitive issues. There are those who say, "What I do with my body is my business." But this is not scriptural. If we have been joined to Christ, what we do with our bodies is the business of the covenant community, because everyone is hurt and offended when the name of Christ is dragged through the gutter or when the name of the church is brought to open shame.

The text prescribes that we go to the offending person. Notice that the ultimate goal is not to condemn but to win the person over. If going alone does not accomplish the goal, we are to take a few others along. This low-key approach keeps the matter from getting widespread distribution, but additional witnesses address the concern that it might be a personal dispute, one person against another. Whereas the offending person might not listen to one person, he or she might heed the words and advice of another.

Taking the matter before the church is a last resort, but it is sometimes necessary, and it is never easy. Nevertheless, while still loving and caring for the offending person, again there is an obligation to uphold the standards and protect the reputation of the church.

Outdated though it may seem to some, there is a time and place for those who are hurting the church to be disfellowshiped. The church must be willing to face the offending person openly and publicly. As painful as this might be, there are times when this is the only way to restore the freedom of the Spirit in the church. In fact, there are more than a few folk who would "straighten up and fly right" if they knew they would have to face an honest brother or sister before the congregation.

While the church must sometimes take a strict stance, it should always be open to the possibility, indeed the hope, of repentance. When repentance has taken place, there must be genuine forgiveness, with no strings attached. This can be difficult if the offensive acts were particularly injurious to individuals or to the church. We've heard people say, "I can forgive, but I can't forget." But for the church, the real issue is reconciliation and restoration of the relationship. We have received reconciliation in abundant measure, and it is not our place to set the limits on forgiveness.

In considering the question of church discipline, we would do well to keep the larger context of this passage from

Matthew in mind. Matthew 18:15-18 deals specifically with the discipline of a member who has become unruly. But the outer boundaries of this passage address larger issues, including the importance of having Christ in our midst.

Even when we face the sensitive issues surrounding church discipline, Jesus is with us, calling us to resolve our differences and be of one accord. But this unity must be rooted in truth and based on standards. It's good to have a full church, but sometimes the spirits will be contrary and the numbers will have to be cut. Even if only two or three are gathered together in his name, he promises to be in their midst.

For Reflection and Discussion

- How have you experienced times when you were able to resolve a conflict, or address a misunderstanding by talking it out? Who took the initiative?
- In what ways does it make a difference in resolving a conflict to bring in a few others whose motives and judgments we trust?
- What do you feel should be the borderline when it comes to behavior or attitudes that require the church to take action?
- Should the church maintain any form of contact with someone who has been disfellowshiped? If so, how?

≡ 24 ≡

Live to the Glory of God

Lesson: 1 Peter 2:9-12

But you are a chosen people, a royal priesthood, a holy nation, a people belonging to God, that you may declare the praises of him who called you out of darkness into his wonderful light. Once you were not a people, but now you are the people of God; once you had not received mercy, but now you have received mercy. (1 PETER 2:9-10, NIV)

➤◢

"We further engage ... through life, amid evil report, and good report, to seek to live to the glory of God."

This phrase as we approach the end of the Covenant focuses on our chief purpose for living: to glorify God. We are called to glorify God amid good and evil report.

Perhaps the most common form of evil report is to be falsely accused or misrepresented. We have all been there at one time or another. We can identify with C. A. Tindley's hymn, "Stand by Me," in which he beseeches, "When I've done the best I can, and my friends misunderstand, ... stand by me."

We must bear in mind the oft-repeated point in the epistles of Peter that the ephemeral circumstances through which believers pass must not determine their outlook in life or their uplook toward God. He addressed his admonition to the churches in Pontus, Galatia, Cappaddocia, Asia, and Bithynia, calling them "strangers." That is, they were not at home in a world that is no friend to grace and that persecutes those who have faith in Christ and commitment to pronounce the gospel. Acknowledging the trials of their faith, he urged them to maintain a lively hope rooted in the resurrection of Jesus Christ. Being treated well by the world was not to deceive them, for those who live godly lives must suffer persecution. Indeed, his argument was that suffering for Christ is a form of purification that refined them like gold.

Jesus declares that there is a state of blessedness when people revile us, persecute us, and say all manner of evil against us falsely for the sake of Christ (Matthew 5:10). It may come as little comfort when we are going through tough times, but the condition we call evil may well be the context in which we are molded and shaped according to the will of God. There is ample biblical support for this notion. Joseph, for instance, was sold into slavery. What his brothers meant for evil, God meant for good. In the case of the man born blind, the disciples debated the cause, asking who sinned, whether it was the man or his parents. Jesus rejected the whole line of discussion with the curious observation that his circumstance was so that God might be glorified (John 9:3). It is true that all things work together for the good of those who love the Lord, for those who are called according to God's purpose (Romans 8:28).

Strange as it may sound, it may be difficult for some people to glorify God when the report is a good one. That is, there are those who can glorify God when times are hard but not when the burdens are lifted. In the midst of the storm they cry out to the Master of the waves, but when the storm has ceased they want to take credit for the powers that have caused it to subside or pretend they can calm the next storm that comes their way.

It is not bad times, after all, but success that might prompt a man to leave the wife who struggled with him and bore their babies when they were poor, or the wife to leave the husband who was by her side before she became famous. Basking in the glitter has led many a child to be ashamed of the parents who nurtured him or her. The lure of worldly success has even caused some preachers to exchange the story of redemption for schemes to achieve material wealth. We would do well to remember the words of our hymn "Lift Every Voice and Sing," wherein the prayer is for the God of our weary years and silent tears to keep us forever in the path, lest our feet stray from the places where we met God, lest the wine of the world intoxicate us so we forget the one who brought us this far.

What we do for the glory of God is the decisive factor, not whether the report is good or evil. The true source of freedom for the believer is that life is lived to the glory of God, that our ultimate allegiance is to the one who has brought us out of darkness into the marvelous light. When we glorify God we return the glory that has been vested with us by virtue of our creation. There is no higher vocation that we can have. Nothing is more excellent than the privilege of returning glory to God. In the midst of our suffering and all our failings, God restores us and permits us to return the glory!

What a relief it should be that we need not seek or receive glory for ourselves and that our stature is not measured by the amount of glory that comes our way! Our vocation to glorify God relieves us to live without being overly concerned about what others think of us and what notoriety we receive. What tremendous freedom this affords young people to realize that when all is said and done what matters is whether God is glorified. This is the perfect remedy for peer pressure and a host of trivial concerns that potentially keep us drained of our energy and missing our focus in life.

No glory can be compared with the glory of those who have been redeemed, brought out of darkness into the marvelous light. For this is the glory to which God is bringing all of creation. In the end, only what is done for the glory of God has lasting value. Everything else fades, loses its luster, and becomes tarnished. The epistle writer put it correctly: "The world passeth away, and the lust thereof: but he that doeth the will of God abideth for ever" (1 John 2:17).

⌖

For Reflection and Discussion

- Do you find it easier to glorify God amid an evil report or a good one? Why?
- How have you or people you know glorified God in bad times and also in good?
- "Only what is done for the glory of the Lord has lasting value." In what ways does this concept give you freedom?

≡ 25 ≡

Unite with Some Church

Lessons: Matthew 16:13-20; Acts 27:27-44

And Simon Peter answered and said, Thou art the Christ, the Son of the living God. And Jesus answered and said unto him, Blessed art thou, Simon Bar-jona: for flesh and blood hath not revealed it unto thee, but my Father which is in heaven. And I say also unto thee, That thou art Peter, and upon this rock I will build my church; and the gates of hell shall not prevail against it. (Matthew 16:16-17)

➤.➤

"When we remove from this place, we engage as soon as possible to unite with some other church where we can carry out the spirit of this covenant and the principles of God's word."

The closing words of the Covenant anticipate the tendency of many to loosen or lose ties that bind them to a Christian community when they relocate. This can happen more easily than we might think. Adjusting to a new set of people can be difficult. The emotional expenditures of parting and the investments required to establish new relationships ought not be underestimated. Some people who relocate procrastinate in their efforts to find a new church. Or they have unrealistic expectations of a new congregation, perhaps comparing it with the one they left. Without a connection to a body of believers, faith can become weak, and we can take liberties with spiritual disciplines that have been a source of strength and stability. Thus the Covenant ends by bringing us to a vow that affirms the necessity of the church.

The Scripture passage from Acts dramatizes this necessity through the metaphor of a ship. The apostle encouraged all on board to remain. The scene is a chaotic one; the ship had been torn apart by an angry sea. The waves of the storm had beaten it to the point of disintegration. Some people were ready to jump overboard, but Paul called out and calmed them. The angel of the Lord appeared to him, letting him know that no one on board the ship would be lost. His admonition was to prevent them from jumping overboard to their destruction rather than remaining in the vessel and being kept safe.

It is tempting to leave the ship and charge into the angry waters when the storm is fierce. Fierce storms have a way of leaving us disoriented to the point where we cannot clearly see what is in our best interest. Surely we have seen this in persons who, in their time of stress, turn against the one who can do them the most good—the one who has cared and has stood by their side. We see it in the church as well. Often when going through troubles people will neglect spending time in worship and fellowship with other believers.

The spirit of the Covenant and the principles of God's Word encourage us to remain on board, to stay in communion within the body of Christ. Many of us have learned early enough that we need the church, even if it does at times seem like a storm-tossed ship. We have believed the promise of protection if we abide in the ship. We can say to our souls with confidence, "The Lord will make a way." Affirming our vows of commitment on calm seas is crucial, for often there is the temptation to jump ship in times of crisis.

While the Covenant highlights relocation, the principle it advocates applies to other critical junctures in life: marriage, childbirth, reaching a new stage of maturity, going away to school, changing jobs, times of sickness and stress. Often, as a result of these critical junctures, we realign habits and priorities, and the church can be left out. A trick of the Enemy is to make us think we don't have the time or energy to make the investment the church requires. We forget what the fellowship of the church gives to us.

By implication, the Covenant upholds a commitment not to a local church body but to the church universal. Based on the theology and purposes of the church explored throughout the Covenant, what more do we need to convince us of our need for it? The church is given by God as the body of Christ in the world and as the bearer of the Spirit. The church is called out from the world to fulfill the promises to Abraham and the vocation of Israel. Through it, all the families of the earth are to be blessed (Romans 9-11). It is the body of Christ through which the grace of God is extended to those who are being saved. The Spirit proceeds through the church to unite those who believe on the Lord Jesus, to regenerate those who repent of their sin, to sanctify all who would grow in grace, and to empower those who would be faithful servants of Christ.

The church stands between the creation and the gates of hell, restraining the mystery of iniquity that threatens at every moment to overtake human history (2 Thessalonians 2:7-10). The promise was not an idle one when the Lord founded the church with the assurance that the gates of hell would not prevail against it. The church takes a stand in favor of values that keep society from crumbling. One can only shudder at the thought of a world without the influence of the church, a world already prone to genocide against ethnic enemies, callous social policy that despises the poor, wanton violence that decimates communities, and flagrant disregard for principles of decency. Dare we deny the safe haven to those we love?

We deceive ourselves if we think we can live and flourish without the church. Yet sometimes we try. Sometimes it is a result of young people staking their claim to independence. Many of us remember as children being made to go to church. There was no referendum; Sunday—all day—was for church. Even when we got big and bad enough to do our stuff on Saturday night, it had nothing to do with whether we would go to church on Sunday. And so some of us vowed in strident tones not to set our foot in church as soon as we got old enough to decide on our own. That is why some people when they leave home also leave the church.

Little did we know what was waiting for us in life. For a few days we behaved like the popular song enjoined: "Be young, be foolish, be happy." We didn't realize that foolishness and happiness are set on a collision course and that it's only a matter of time before foolishness turns happiness into emptiness. Emptiness turns into meaninglessness and despair. There are dead ends in life from which the only escape is the deliverance God has provided in the church. The course of the fool leads to loneliness, for which God has made provision in the fellowship of believers.

Life is not meant to be lived in isolation or by individuals whose only goal is to do their own thing. If we rear our children that way, they will not be able to cope with the crises they shall surely face. Living as God intends is more than being surrounded by mother, father, and children. It is more than being in a circle of blood relations. It takes a community to rear children and to give them the spiritual resources for living productive lives that bring glory to God.

A good dose of life brought many baby boomers back to the church. In attempting to nurture children, many boomers realized the value of much of what they had received as children. In fact, what was given in Sunday school had grounded them for life. The opportunities to exercise leadership, given in the church, gave the confidence needed for the challenges they faced. Like prodigals, many boomers came back to mothers and fathers in the church who were waiting with open arms. Some are still coming back and are looking for the signal that they are still welcome. We who have remained must make sure they receive such a sign.

The church is a gift from God, an instrument through which we learn God's truth, experience God's presence, find the support we need, and offer the support others need. We honor the giving of the gift of the church by pledging always to be a part of it, no matter the circumstances.

➤◼◀

For Reflection and Discussion

- In what ways has the church provided you with spiritual and emotional grounding?
- Have there been times in your life when you have forgotten about the church? What were those times like? What did you miss? What brought you back?
- Are there good reasons some people fall away from the church? What can be done to limit this from happening?

Select Bibliography

Baldwin, Lewis V. *There Is a Balm in Gilead: The Cultural Roots of Martin Luther King.* Minneapolis: Fortress Press, 1991. Looks beyond King's intellectual lift to explore the currents within the milieu of the African American life and religion that shaped one of the most significant figures of the twentieth century.

————. *To Make the Wounded Whole: The Cultural Legacy of Martin Luther King, Jr.* Minneapolis: Fortress Press, 1992. Continues the crucial study of King, showing the impact of African American culture in shaping King's mind and public ministry.

Cannon, Katie G. *Black Womanist Ethics.* Atlanta: Scholars Press, 1988. A discussion of how race, gender, and class are complementary factors in an adequate analysis of the African American situation, prodding black theology to expand its analytical grid in light of black female experience.

Clemmons, Ithiel C. Bishop C. H. *Mason and the Roots of the Church of God in Christ.* Bakersfield, Calif.: Pneuma Life Publications, 1996. A study of the emergence and growth of the largest black Pentecostal denomination in the United States. Attention is given to the contribution of African American spirituality to the Christian church.

Cone, James H. *Black Theology and Black Power.* New York: Seabury Press, 1969. Demonstrates the commensurability of Black Power, a sociopolitical movement of the late 1960s, with the gospel. In contrast with King's emphasis on redemptive suffering, Cone suggests revolutionary violence as an option for achieving liberation.

———. *A Black Theology of Liberation*. Philadelphia: Lippincott, 1970. A systematic theology for African American Christians, making the experience of African Americans a focal point of the theology and exposing the so-called biblical and theological foundations of racism.

———. *For My People: Black Theology and the Black Church*. Maryknoll, N.Y.: Orbis Books, 1984. Traces the development of Cone's thought as he enters into dialogue with early critics and roots his work more clearly in the religious experience of African American Christians.

———. *God of the Oppressed*. New York: Seabury Press, 1975. Probes how concern for the oppressed is central in the experience and theological reflection of the African American church. These interests properly belong at the outset of a relevant and responsible theological project.

Fisher, Miles Mark. *Negro Slave Songs in the United States*. Ithaca, N.Y.: Cornell University Press for the American Historical Association, 1953. With a foreword by Ray Allen Billington. A classic study of how African slaves expressed their faith and passion for freedom in lyrical verse. Argued that the songs were not only expressions of faith but encoded strategies and plans for escape.

Fitts, Leroy. *A History of Black Baptists*. Nashville: Broadman Press, 1985. An attempt to give historical context for the Baptist movement among African Americans. Considerable attention is given to the role of associations and conventions in the movement.

Forbes, James A., Jr. *The Holy Spirit and Preaching*. Nashville:

Abingdon, 1989. Examines the work of the Holy Spirit in the preparation and delivery of the sermon, especially in the African American church culture. A singular contribution to pneumatology, a field of theology largely neglected by black theologians.

Frazier, Edward Franklin, and C. Eric Lincoln. *The Negro Church in America* and *The Black Church Since Frazier*. New York: Schocken Books, 1974. Part I is the classic study of the Negro church by Frazier, accounting for initial conversions and the development of institutional religion among Negroes in the United States. Part II is Lincoln's update, showing the influence of the civil rights and Black Power movements that had a radical impact on the black church during the second half of the twentieth century.

Gavins, Raymond. *The Perils and Prospects of Southern Black Leadership: Gordon Blaine Hancock, 1884–1970*. Durham, N.C.: Duke University Press, 1993. A behind-the-scenes look at the black scholars, educators, publishers, and activists who advanced the cause of social justice in the early twentieth century. A particular focus on the work of Hancock in the Southern Regional Council.

Grant, Jacquelyn. *White Women's Christ and Black Women's Jesus: Feminist Christology and Womanist Response*. Atlanta: Scholars Press, 1989. Explores the limits of classical Christology in light of the feminist critique. Further examines feminist critique in light of black female experience, introducing the categories of race and class and how they influence the African American female.

Harris, James H. *Pastoral Theology: A Black-Church Perspective*. Minneapolis: Fortress Press, 1991. The practice of ministry within the African American church is brought to light as a required subfield in an adequate treatment of black theology. Attention is given to the distinct challenges facing the black pastor.

————. *Preaching Liberation*. Minneapolis: Fortress Press, 1995. A study in homiletics that applies insights of black theology for the purpose of achieving a liberative focus.

Hicks, H. Beecher, Jr. *Preaching Through a Storm*. Grand Rapids, Mich.: Zondervan Publishing House, 1987. With a foreword by William A. Jones. A collection of sermons that illustrates how preaching guides and forms the church as it goes through crises.

Hiscox, Edward Thurston. *The Hiscox Standard Baptist Manual*. Valley Forge, Pa.: Judson Press, 1965. The unsurpassed Baptist church directory, this manual is a guide to the doctrines, discipline, officers, ordinances, principles, and practices of Baptist churches.

Hopkins, Dwight, and George Cummings, eds. *Cut Loose Your Stammering Tongue: Black Theology in the Slave Narratives*. Maryknoll, N.Y.: Orbis Books, 1991. An exercise in exploring the literary efforts of African Americans as a source of black theology. This is an alternative to excessive reliance on European and Euro-American theologians.

Hudson, Winthrop S., and Norman H. Maring, eds. *A Baptist Manual of Polity and Practice*. Valley Forge, Pa.: Judson Press, 1991. Basic volume that illustrates the relationship of Baptist beliefs to the larger Protestant movement and supplies an overview of Baptist history in the U.S. Includes the confessions and covenants critical to understanding Baptist faith and order.

King, Martin Luther, Jr. *Stride Toward Freedom: The Montgomery Story*. New York: Harper, 1958. An account of the early civil rights movement by the chief architect. The theological and philosophical underpinnings are probed to show how this nonviolent movement is the embodiment of the Christian response.

———. *Where Do We Go from Here: Chaos or Community?* New York: Harper & Row, 1967. One of King's later writings that analyzed the racist dogmas and behaviors that pervaded the South, breeding violence and poverty. Affirms the analysis and positive intent of "Black Power," but argues against the use of such language.

Küng, Hans. *The Church.* Translated by Ray and Rosaleen Ockenden. London: Burns & Oates, 1968. An essay on ecclesiology from one of the foremost Roman Catholic theologians that seeks to comprehend the institutional and congregational sides of church life. Extremely helpful for exploring how the dimensions of the church's life are held in tension.

LaRue, Cleophus J. *The Heart of Black Preaching.* Louisville: Westminster John Knox Press, 2000. A study of black preaching, looking at characteristic motifs in the preaching tradition. Examines sermons selected for insight into currents that guided the African American church to a prophetic posture.

Lincoln, C. Eric, and Lawrence H. Mamiya, *The Black Church in the African-American Experience.* Durham, N.C.: Duke University Press, 1990. One of the few statistical surveys of the black church. Provides brief histories of and basic facts and figures for the seven historically black denominations.

Lincoln, C. Eric, ed. *The Black Experience in Religion.* Garden City, N.Y.: Anchor Press, 1974. A collection of essays that give an overview of African American religion.

———. *The Black Muslims in America.* Boston: Beacon Press, 1973. The classic study that brought the Nation of Islam to the attention of the American Academy and the U.S. as a whole. Illustrates the link between the various religious alternatives among African Americans and their possible responses to the experience of racism and oppression.

———. *Coming Through the Fire: Surviving Race and Place in America*. Durham, N.C.: Duke University Press, 1996. An autobiography chronicling Lincoln's experiences from his childhood in Alabama to the pinnacle of his career as a professor and scholar.

Mays, Benjamin, *The Negro's God as Reflected in His Literature*. Boston: Chapman & Grimes, Inc., 1938. Examination of sermons, addresses, and writings of black clergy and religious leaders who were forerunners of the modern civil rights, Black Power, and black theology movements.

———, and Joseph W. Nicholson. *The Negro's Church*. New York: Russell & Russell, 1969. One of the earliest empirical studies of the black church, examining the denominational patterns and showing the population to have been primarily Baptist, Methodist, and Holiness. This ground-breaking work provided the basis for subsequent sociological analyses.

McClendon, James William. *Systematic Theology*. Nashville: Abingdon Press, 1986. An attempt at developing a narrative theology from the Baptist perspective.

Moltmann, Jürgen. *The Church in the Power of the Spirit: A Contribution to Messianic Ecclesiology*. Translated by Margaret Kohl. New York: Harper & Row, 1977. One in a series of classic volumes in systematic theology by one of the foremost theologians of the twentieth century. Uses the doctrine of the Trinity as the starting point for developing an ecclesiology that identifies social justice for the oppressed as a key mission of the church.

Newbigin, Lesslie. *Foolishness to the Greeks: The Gospel and Western Culture*. Grand Rapids, Mich.: W. B. Eerdmans,

1986. Discussion of how the gospel challenges culture and vice versa. Critically assesses the impact of the Enlightenment and scientific thought on human consciousness and the human condition in the modern world.

Proctor, Samuel D. *The Substance of Things Hoped For: A Memoir of African-American Faith*. New York: G. P. Putnam & Sons, 1995. An autobiographical account that traces an African American family's rise from slavery's ashes to worldwide diplomacy. Highlights hope as a critical element in productive living.

————, and Gardner C. Taylor. *We Have This Ministry: The Heart of the Pastor's Vocation*. Valley Forge, Pa.: Judson Press, 1996. Essays by two of the most influential preachers of the twentieth century, examining pastoral ministry in the African American church. Represents the best wisdom of the African American Christian tradition and offers rich insight for the church as a whole.

Roberts, J. Deotis. *Liberation and Reconciliation: A Black Theology*. Maryknoll, N.Y.: Orbis Books, 1994. An examination of the two essential categories—liberation and reconciliation—that must be kept in tension for black theology to be Christian theology. Keeps the experience of ordinary Christians within the larger theological dialogue about issues of racism and oppression.

————. *The Prophethood of Black Believers: An African-American Political Theology for Ministry*. Louisville: Westminster/John Knox Press, 1994. Explores issues that must be raised if the African American church is to maintain a prophetic voice in the twenty-first century, both within and beyond the black church community.

————, and James J. Gardner, eds. *Quest for a Black Theology*. Philadelphia: Pilgrim Press, 1971. A collection of essays by black scholars and theologians that proved instrumental in shaping the subfield of black theology as it emerged. These essays proved crucial for establishing language and supplying early dialogue.

Sanders, Cheryl. *Saints in Exile: The Holiness-Pentecostal Experience in African American Religion and Culture*. New York: Oxford University Press, 1996. An examination of the Church of God (Anderson, Indiana), a Holiness denomination, in relation to black evangelical bodies. A crucial study for understanding Holiness-Pentecostalism as part of the larger black church movement.

Sanneh, Lamin O. *Abolitionists Abroad: American Blacks and the Making of Modern West Africa*. Cambridge, Mass.: Harvard University Press, 1999. A study of how the efforts of African American Christians who returned to West Africa transformed the missionary enterprise and set the stage for modern missions.

Smith, H. Shelton. *In His Image, But...: Racism in Southern Religion*. Durham, N.C.: Duke University Press, 1972. A study of the proslavery argument that was advanced on theological grounds. Essential reading for those who would comprehend the theological roots of modern racism.

Sobel, Mechal. *Trabelin' On: The Slave Journey to an Afro-Baptist Faith*. Westport, Conn.: Greenwood Press, 1979. Traces the roots of black Baptist faith within Protestantism and the worldview of African religions.

Sobrino, Jon. *The True Church and the Poor*. Translated from the Spanish by Matthew J. O'Connell. London: SCM Press, 1985. Ecclesiology developed by a Latin American Roman Catholic liberation theologian that explores the meaning of the church as "one, holy, catholic, and apostolic" in the face of late-twentieth-century struggles with poverty and power.

Taylor, Gardner C. *How Shall They Preach?* Elgin: Progressive Convention Press, 1977. A collection of sermons by one of the greatest preachers of the twentieth century. Taylor illustrates how careful reading and interpretation of the biblical text fires imagination in the black preaching tradition.

Thurman, Howard. *Jesus and the Disinherited.* New York: Abingdon-Cokesbury Press, 1949. Seminal study of the gospel tradition that highlights ministry of Jesus among the poor and his concern with their plight. In terms of this book's effect on King and others of his generation, one might say it is a "Proto-Black Theology."

Washington, James Melvin. *Frustrated Fellowship: The Black Baptist Quest for Social Power.* Macon, Ga.: Mercer, 1986. A technical and detailed historical study of the efforts of black Baptists to retain fellowship with the larger Baptist fellowship. Charts their limited success and the creation of their own African American associations.

Washington, Joseph. *Black Religion: The Negro and Christianity in the United States.* Boston: Beacon Press, 1966. Emphasis is placed on the importance of conversion experience and the significance of protest as characteristic features of African American faith. This study sparked critical responses that led to what became known as black theology and black church studies.

West, Cornel. *Prophesy Deliverance! An Afro-American Revolutionary Christianity.* Philadelphia: Westminster Press, 1982. An examination of a prophetic posture in history as the key to African American Christian spirituality. Outlines the emergence of racism in the modern world, against which the Afro-Christian prophetic posture can be viewed.

———. *Race Matters.* New York: Vintage Books, 1994. Explores how race shapes modern discourse even when it is not named, often interfering with relevant analysis that necessarily requires use of other critical categories, such as gender, class, and economic issues.

Woodson, Carter G. *The History of the Negro Church*. Washington: Associated Publishers, 1972. One of the first attempts to give a historical account of the religious life of African Americans. Traces the development from early contacts between Africans and evangelical Christians to the development of independent movements, laying the foundation for further studies.

Wilmore, Gayraud S., ed. *African American Religious Studies: An Interdisciplinary Anthology*. Durham, N.C.: Duke University Press, 1989. A collection of articles by some of the finest scholars in the African American community, covering a range of religious and theological topics. A must for anyone who would be knowledgeable in the field of black religious studies.